PENGUIN A

SHIVA

Nityanand Charan Das is a practising monk at the Sri Sri Radha Gopinath Temple, ISKCON Chowpatty, Mumbai, and a visionary who wishes to revolutionize the current urban scenario by helping people live a life of purpose, fulfilment and satisfaction. He specializes in guiding today's youth to reconnect with their roots and lead a simple yet happy life.

Coming from an army background, Nityanand Charan Das's childhood desire was to become an army officer. However, Lord Krishna had other plans for him and orchestrated his life beautifully. Life led him to fail the National Defence Academy (NDA) interview, despite being one of the best in the group; he took up engineering instead, and eventually became a monk when he was just twenty-four years old.

Nityanand Charan Das focuses on making the sacred teachings of our holy scriptures simple so that they resonate with anyone and everyone. His message is simple: 'Spiritual life is not a life of rejection. It is a life of connection.' He says, we do not have to give up anything, we simply have to add this valuable dimension to our life.

His divine radiance can be felt far and wide: his discourses are heard in every major city in India and in more than fifty countries across the globe.

ncd.rns@gmail.com
http://www.nityanandcharandas.com/
https://instagram.com/nityananda_charan_das
https://www.facebook.com/NityanandCharanD
https://www.facebook.com/Nityanand.Caran.Das

SHIVA

The Hidden Side of
the Master of the Universe

NITYANAND
CHARAN DAS

PENGUIN
ANANDA

An imprint of Penguin Random House

PENGUIN ANANDA

Penguin Ananda is an imprint of the Penguin Random House group of
companies whose addresses can be found at global.penguinrandomhouse.com

Published by Penguin Random House India Pvt. Ltd
4th Floor, Capital Tower 1, MG Road,
Gurugram 122 002, Haryana, India

Penguin
Random House
India

First published in Penguin Ananda by Penguin Random House India 2024

ISBN 9780143467441

Typeset in Minion Pro by MAP Systems, Bengaluru, India
Printed at Replika Press Pvt. Ltd, India

www.penguin.co.in

MIX
Paper | Supporting
responsible forestry
FSC™ C016779

To the great Sage Vyasa, the original compiler of all the Vedic texts that serve as a guiding light for all humanity

Contents

Foreword   ix

Introduction   xiii

  1. The Auspicious One   1
  2. The Origin of Lord Shiva   5
  3. Shaivism vs Vaishnavism   13
  4. The Identity of Lord Shiva   19
  5. The Birth of Lord Shiva   29
  6. Goddess Parvati: The Universal
     Mother   32
  7. The Birth of Kartikeya: The Mighty
     Commander   37
  8. The Birth of Lord Ganesh   44
  9. Kailash   52
 10. Shivaratri: The Night of Lord Shiva   60
 11. Rudraksha: The Sacred Bead   63
 12. Bel Patra: The Sacred Leaf   66
 13. Varanasi: The Capital of Lord Shiva   70
 14. The Legend of Amarnath   88

15. Different Roles   93

16. History of the Twelve Jyotirlingas   113

    1. Somnath   113
    2. Mallikarjuna   118
    3. Mahakaleshwar   122
    4. Omkareshwar   125
    5. Kedarnath   127
    6. Bhimashankar   130
    7. Vishwanath   133
    8. Trimbakeshwar   135
    9. Baidyanath   143
  10. Nageshwar   146
  11. Rameshwar   150
  12. Grishneshwar   152

17. Lord Shiva in Vrindavan   157

    1. Bhuteshvara Mahadeva   157
    2. Gopishvar Mahadeva   158
    3. Kameshvara Mahadeva   161
    4. Chakaleshvar Mahadeva   162
    5. Nandishvar Mahadeva   162

18. Lord Shiva Gives the Best   168

19. The Lover of Bhagavat   171

20. Shivastak: A Beautiful Prayer   174

21. Rudra Gita   179

22. Vaishnavas' Worship of Lord Shiva   205

23. The Secret Shiva   214

Acknowledgements   221

Foreword

The winds of grace are always blowing, but it is you who must raise your sails. By staying open to the beauty around us, we can experience unexpected moments of grace. When we have faith in our journey instead of just hoping for the best, we can be surprised by where life takes us. As a Shiva devotee, I understand the true meaning of divine intervention. Every time I faced big changes and challenges in life, I saw God's handiwork in them. Although I certainly could not find it at any of those times, I can now see that everything has worked out for the best. These incidents have the power to alter the journey of our life.

It's heart-warming to know that Prabhuji feels blessed to have Lord Krishna in his life, and acknowledges that this divine presence is a precious gift from Lord Shiva.

It's true and I have faced this a million times, when people compare Shaivism and Vaishnavism. In my opinion, Shaivism and Vaishnavism are like two wings of the same bird, working in harmony to achieve balance and stability within the universe. Both these practices have their unique strengths. One cannot exist without the other. Unity in religions is achieved by achieving unity in the philosophies, knowing that all are teaching the same subject. But as per as the capacity of the respective students to digest, the meagre difference in the cultures can no longer stand as a separating factor. I have achieved unity in philosophies by reading and understanding, and through conversations with people such as Nityanand ji.

I remember, years ago, a work trip led me to Indore and then to Ujjain, where I visited the Shri Mahakaleshwar Temple, one of the most prominent and holy sites of Lord Shiva. The energy of this place was unlike anything I had ever felt before. I decided to sit down and meditate there. Something started happening to me, but I didn't really understand what it was. It was happening more on an energetic and spiritual level. Instead of being scared, I welcomed it and gave it space to be. What I experienced was incredible.

I am sure the readers will feel a deep connection as they read this book. How everything in life (including Lord Krishna and Shiva) is connected has been beautifully explained by Prabhuji. Lord Shiva has a special position in Vedic heritage. His aspiration to participate in the *rasa lila* is a beautiful story that has also been narrated.

Throughout my spiritual journey, I have come across many *bhakti Shaivites* and *jnana yogis* who worship Lord Vishnu.

While Vaishnavism is usually associated with bhakti (loving devotional service) and karma yoga, Shaivism is more closely linked with jnana and *kriya* yoga. However, those who are mature will easily understand the deep purpose of Lord Shiva within this universe—to gradually uplift even the most unqualified to the ultimate platform of spiritual perfection. But that is something I would like to leave for the readers to discover in the pages of this sacred work. In other words, we cannot be a devotee of Lord Krishna if we neglect Lord Shiva and we cannot truly love Lord Shiva without loving Lord Krishna. The in-depth knowledge of Prabhu Nityanandji helps us understand how closely related they are.

All human beings have been blessed by the Supreme Lord with the free will to make choices, and when more is given, more is expected. Sinful souls require the boundless mercy of a higher power to compassionately lift them up. Lord Shiva uplifts such downtrodden creatures through his presence and association. Despite associating with such inauspicious beings, He remains pure. The connection between Lord Shiva and Lord Krishna/Lord Vishnu is such that Krishna is the heart of Shiva, and Shiva is the heart of Krishna. Words are not enough to describe the relationship between Lord Krishna and Lord Shiva but Prabhuji has done this extremely well. So strong is the bond between Lord Krishna and Lord Shiva that they cannot live without each other. Shiva is known as Naṭarāja, the king of dance, and Krishna is known as Raṅga-nātha, the king of the world stage.

Leading someone towards eternal God-consciousness is indeed a work of the greatest welfare. However, it is not an easy task. Additionally, throughout history, those who have dedicated themselves to this work have often been persecuted. People are not persecuted by accident or because of their karma. They experience hardships and suffering because of their devotion to Krishna. Through their willingness to accept any consequences, they demonstrate their commitment to spreading Krishna's glory and helping others who are suffering. Lord Krishna and Lord Shiva are both known for demonstrating the depth of a devotee's devotion. Lord Shiva demonstrated this in various ways, such as drinking the poison Halahala to save humanity, or destroying Tripuras, the three floating castle cities made of steel, silver and gold built by Maya for the Asuras. Lord Shiva is considered the greatest guardian of karma.

Lord Shiva loves those who are devoted to the Supreme Lord Krishna. The devotees must always know that Lord Krishna is the Supreme Lord and that Lord Shiva is his devotee. In His pastimes, we see the Supreme Lord (as Lord Ram) worshipping Shiva frequently.

As an artist, I appreciate the way that art and theology depict the philosophical and spiritual concepts present in *harihara*. Harihara symbolizes the unity between Krishna and Shiva, representing the harmonious coexistence of diverse beliefs within one.

A faithful retelling of Lord Shiva's account, this book reads as a story of who, what and how, and starts with Prabhuji's journey—his exceptionally curious childhood and tales of Lord Shiva.

Thank you, Prabhuji, for writing such a wonderful account. Each one of us has a divine light that is encoded in our being, waiting to be awakened. The totality of this beautiful creation is experienced as divine ecstasy in the hearts of humanity.

Happy reading and a joyful life to all seekers.

—Rouble Nagi
Social worker, artist and author of *The Slum Queen*

Introduction

Throughout my upbringing, Lord Shiva has consistently held a place as a predominant deity in my life. Himachal Pradesh, also known as Devabhoomi (the land of the celestial gods), is a northern Indian state known for the simplicity of its people's lives. Unlike the modern world, the state is still quite well established in its ancient traditions, where people seem to be satisfied with the bare minimum. They are God-fearing, simple-hearted and sincere in their worship of their respective deities; primarily Lord Shiva, various forms of Goddess Durga and local village deities. The state also boasts of being home to various prominent sites where Lord Shiva and Durga are worshipped, known as *shakti peethas*.

The environment in my humble house was no different. As I was told, my grandfather, a veteran of World War II, was a worshipper of Goddess Durga. She blessed him with powers, owing to the mercy of his Guru, with whom he did his sadhana quite early in the morning. My father imbibed a similar dedication. I saw him, my mother and other family members (since I lived in a joint family) religiously dedicating a significant amount of time in the day to their spiritual practices. These practices were primarily centred on offering prayers and articles of worship like incense and lamps filled with cotton wicks soaked in ghee to the framed pictures of Lord Shiva and Mother Parvati (another name for Goddess Durga). As my childhood, the most impressionable age, was spent witnessing such sincere dedication to the deities, I subconsciously picked it up too.

I grew up as a God-fearing person and was always very particular about reciting my prayers daily and offering my worship as taught by my father. Any temple I would see, I had to offer my respects, at times repeatedly as I feared if I did not do it properly, the deities in the temple would get angry and as a result, I might lose my next cricket match or not get good marks in my exams. Obviously, this was not the best consciousness to have—to drag the deities to our level of thinking, as if they would get upset if not offered proper respect. We humans can think like that. We feel bad when someone does not pay us respect, but deities like Lord Shiva and Mother Parvati are not like us. They are extremely evolved personalities, free from envy and desires for personal adoration or distinction. But as the saying goes—we see others as we are, not as they are. So we try to impose our consciousness on such exalted personalities as well, who are extremely kind and non-judgemental.

This fear kept me glued to my daily worship of Lord Shiva, irrespective of where or with whom I stayed. I had friends who had every type of bad habit, but this divine connection and the fear of being punished in some way if I indulged in any misdeed proved to be a great and decisive deterrent in the long run. I managed to not pick up any of their bad habits. It also instilled a sort of courage in me that there was someone always there to protect me if I faced any challenges. So I was fearful of them internally but had a kind of fearless disposition towards the outside world. By some unjustified grace and due to the strong spiritual foundation in my childhood, I could remain consistent in my mode of worship to Lord Shiva and Goddess Parvati/Durga. All through this, I simply worshipped Lord Shiva, honestly without expecting anything (though I childishly did ask him for a few materialistic things). But the prominent feeling while worshipping him that remained was simply awe and reverence. The connection became stronger through my school days and college life as well, for exactly twenty-three years.

Despite all this, every now and then, even though I was leading a happy life, a thought would pop up, 'Something seems to be missing in life. I do not know what it is, but there is some sort of vacuum.' The thought would spontaneously show up and grab my attention for a few seconds, and then it would disappear. Sometimes, I would be playing a cricket match when it happened. Little did I realize that soon, everything was about to change.

The Turning Point

It was my second year of engineering at Malegaon College of Engineering (MCE), Baramati, when the most prominent aspect of my life went through a complete overhaul.

I was walking with a friend in the city where I studied when I suddenly spotted a bus that had a bookstall at the back. I loved bookstores because I was interested in the mystic Siddhis (Tantra-mantra), and would regularly buy and read books on the topic. I was even looking for a guru in the field who could guide me in my sadhana and help me gain some mystic perfection. So when I saw a bookstall, I was really excited. I ran up to the back of the bus and saw a monk dressed in white sitting at the book table. As I looked at the books, none of them seemed to be interesting. Needless to say, I was terribly disappointed. The only book that caught my attention had a skull on its cover. I thought this might have some tantra-mantra (since we associate skulls with mystics), but when I opened it, it only had verses from the Bhagavad Gita and Shrimad Bhagavatam. I placed the book back down, feeling dejected. The devotee tried to show and convince me to buy a book or two, but my response was, 'Do you have a book on Lord Shiva?' The devotee replied they had none. So I said, 'Then I am not interested.' He tried to show me another book (*The Science of Self-Realization* by Srila Prabhupada, founder Acharya of the International Society for Krishna Consciousness [ISKCON]), which was supposed to be very good for students, but I had already made up my mind to not discuss anything further.

Then next day, the devotees of Lord Krishna from ISKCON visited my college for a seminar on the 'Secret of Happiness'. With initial reluctance, we, a group of friends, decided to attend the seminar and forgo the cricket match that we had planned for the day.

We attended this seminar, but I don't remember assimilating anything from the talk. However, at the end of the seminar, the devotees asked whether anyone would like to attend Gita classes every week. And this was something I had always wanted to do. Every now and then, I would tell myself that I needed to find out what was inside this most revered and famous book, at least once in my lifetime. It was not a very prominent thought, but there was certainly a deep desire. So when this opportunity came up, I wholeheartedly grabbed it.

The Gift from Lord Shiva

The weekly Gita classes started in our cottage inside the college campus. There were a handful of us who eventually started liking these sessions, more so due to the delicious *prasada*[1] that the devotees would offer at the end. We grew closer to Lord Krishna gradually, but I still had a big mental block. I liked Lord Krishna, but I did not want to give up my loyalty towards Lord Shiva. I still very much identified myself as a Lord Shiva devotee. And when *kirtans*[2] would happen, I would not sing or chant like others around. Instead, I would simply close my eyes so I did not have to feel embarrassed when others noticed that I wasn't chanting. I wanted to chant, but somehow I could not.

One evening, the devotees who would come every week for the sessions invited us over to their rented place in the town. We would gather, chant, hear discourses and enjoy a nice feast. It happened to be Ekadashi—a sacred day dedicated to Lord Krishna. We went, thoroughly excited, as we had finally started enjoying this life. In the evening, the kirtan started and I, as usual, closed my eyes and did not open my mouth to sing Lord Krishna's names at all.

---

[1] Food offered to God first.

[2] Devotional chants.

But while I did this, internally, I kept repeating to myself: 'Krishna! I really do want to chant your name but what can I do? I am a Lord Shiva devotee. So I cannot.' After some more kirtan, we had our Ekadashi feast and slept.

In the morning, as we were leaving, the devotee gave me a copy of his old Gita and asked me to read six verses every day (which I religiously did and completed the entire sacred text). This is where the turning point came. As soon as I took the Gita in my hands and opened it, in one go, the page with the following verse opened up mysteriously (10.23):

rudranam shankarash chasmi
vittesho yaksha-rakshasam
vasunam pavakash casmi
meruh shikharinam aham

'Of all the Rudras,[3] I am Lord Shiva,
of the Yakṣas and Rakshasas I am the Lord of wealth [Kuvera], of the Vasus I am fire [Agni], and of mountains I am Meru.'

As soon as I read Lord Krishna telling Arjuna, 'Of all the Rudras, I am Lord Shiva', all the confusion was over and all the reluctance immediately disappeared. It was as if Lord Krishna heard my words the previous night and personally came in the form of the Gita to convince me. There was no looking back after that. However, all this was due to the

---

[3] In the Vedas, *Rudra* is known as the divine archer, who shoots arrows of death and disease and who has to be implored not to slay or injure in his wrath.

grace of Lord Shiva. When he is pleased with us, he gives us what is closest to his heart. And Lord Krishna is certainly someone whom he holds in his heart. Both Lord Shiva and Lord Krishna are inseparable and they have a very close connection. We cannot accept one and reject the other. Wherever we find Lord Krishna's temple, we also find a Lord Shiva temple close by.

I was not the only one who was guided to Lord Krishna by Lord Shiva. Countless souls have received this special gift from him. When we revisit history, we see that great Vaishnava saints, such as Shri Vallabhacharya and Shri Narasingh Mehta, were also led by Lord Shiva to Lord Krishna. Therefore, I believe Lord Krishna in my life is a gift from Lord Shiva for which I eternally remain indebted to him.

This book is a humble attempt to express my deepest gratitude to Lord Shiva—the kindest and most compassionate personality—by revealing his true glory to the whole world.

I humbly pray to Lord Krishna to guide my thoughts and words so that I can do justice to this sacred task of glorifying His favourite associate. May Lord Shiva bless all the readers with what is most dear to their heart. May this be our only wish and prayer, life after life.

Chapter 1

The Auspicious One

Lord Shiva means 'the auspicious one' or 'the one who brings auspiciousness'. So many seem to know of this greatly worshipped, intriguing and mysterious personality but very few actually know the truth about him. Hiding in his own mysticism, Lord Shiva is the personification of power, peace, kindness and love. Universally adored, he seems to be the most non-controversial figure in Vedic history, and is known as Ashutosh, Rudra, Chandramaulishvar, Nandishvar, Bhootnath, Neelkanth, Bholenath, Gangadhar and many more such endearing names.

Executing a variety of duties within the universe and playing multifarious roles, he is the Lord of the material world.

It is not easy to understand his personality—certainly not as easy as people assume. Religion without philosophy is sentimentalism or fanaticism. Hence, it is important to dig deeper into various scriptures, which are the most authentic sources of knowledge when it comes to knowing such great personalities.

Some people wrongly extend the notion that Lord Shiva means 'nothingness' or assert that he is not a distinct personality but rather a state of consciousness. However, whenever we come across any reference to Lord Shiva in any of the scriptures, we always refer to him as a person—his form, his dealings as an individual, his family, his abode and his activities are all described. Someone who is not a person cannot have so many attributes. Even if someone claims that it is 'nothingness' that has taken form, why is it that his personality is emphasized so much everywhere? We talk about his activities and attributes. How can nothingness have such aspects without being a person? Form gives rise to formlessness but it's not true for the opposite, much like the bulb gives rise to light, not the other way around.

An Extraordinary Person

It needs very little common sense to conclude: Lord Shiva is a person, in fact, an extraordinary person, who is beyond our mundane perception. He is a completely spiritual personality and thus, not easy to understand with our blunt material senses. If we wish to understand or know him, we must first accept his personal features (accept him as a person). Otherwise, he reserves the right to remain unknowable. If we do not even believe that he exists in his transcendental form, why should he show his form to us?

Lord Shiva blesses his followers with material opulence but does not even have a house for himself. He is the perfect example of simple living and high thinking. Through his actions, he teaches a very important principle to his followers, who come to him seeking material benedictions—that happiness is not dependent on material opulence. In fact, those who possess such abundance end up leading a life full of anxieties. He is almost mockingly saying, 'All of you come to seek facilities for material enjoyment from me, but look at me! I have the power to create wealth, but I am living without it and I feel completely satisfied because I have got something higher.'

Lord Shiva gives those who worship him with sincere love and without any material motivation, what is closest to his heart. Something that he himself is always absorbed in and always meditating upon. What that secret is will be revealed later in the pages of this book.

Interesting Family

Lord Shiva has the most interesting family. He is known to be the most sober personality i.e with senses under full control, but his wife, Mother Parvati, happens to be none other than Durga or Mayadevi herself, who puts all living beings in the material world under an illusion because of which they lose all control over their senses and become devoid of any power of discrimination. Their children are Lord Ganesh and Kartikeya. Lord Shiva, who carries a snake around his neck, is carried around by Nandi, the bull. Mother Parvati's vehicle is the lion. Lord Ganesh rides on a mouse and Lord Kartikeya travels on a peacock. All of these carriers have different personalities, but they are still together.

Generally, we see that the lion eats the bull, the snake eats the mouse and the peacock eats the snake. But in Lord Shiva's family, all these living entities live in complete harmony.

This illustrious family of Lord Shiva conveys a very important message: each individual is different. Not even twins are the same. There will be differences of opinions wherever we have multiple individuals but if we have a higher purpose in mind and are united in that purpose, then even after having diverse personalities, we can live together happily. But if 'I, me or mine' becomes the focus, then everything falls apart. Each person must discover and embrace their unique higher purpose to live a life of harmony in *Kaliyuga*, the present age of discord and misery. If we centre our family life around God, then we can always live happily ever after. A family that prays together stays together.

Chapter 2

The Origin of Lord Shiva
(Reconciling various Puranic versions)

The divine Sage Vyasa wrote Vedic scriptures, such as the Vedas, Puranas, Upanishads, Mahabharata and the Vedanta Sutra, and if a person goes through all of them, he might get confused about the origin of Lord Shiva. The Shiva Purana describes him as the supreme and the Vishnu Purana describes Lord Krishna/Lord Vishnu as the supreme. Why such contradictions? Wouldn't it have been easier if he just made things crystal clear? After all, there cannot be many Supremes.

Let us understand why the puranic versions differ in some aspects.

Firstly, we have to understand that the Vedic scriptures are reciprocal in terms of the level of consciousness of the seeker.

Lord Krishna says in the Bhagavad Gita (4.11):

> *ye yetha maam prapadyante,*
> *tams tathaiva bhajame aham*

'As all surrender to me, I will reward accordingly.'

Here, what does the reward refer to? It can be many things.

In the Bhagavad Gita (7.21–23), Lord Krishna describes the system of demigod worship:

yo yo yam yam tanum bhaktah
shraddhayarchitum icchati
tasya tasyacalam shraddham
tam eva vidadhamy aham

'I am in everyone's heart as the supersoul (*paramatma*).
As soon as one desires to worship heavenly deities,
I ensure their faith becomes steady, enabling them to
devote themselves to that particular deity.'

How does He ensure this? There are many ways:

1. To begin with, as a supersoul in everyone's heart, He encourages whatever inclination a person has towards a particular *devata* (celestial god).
2. Secondly, He also arranges for them to associate with others who are worshipping that particular deity.
3. Thirdly, He also provides scriptures that glorify that particular devata.

Matsya Purana, the oldest Purana, states that the eighteen Puranas are classified into three modes:

1. The mode of goodness,
2. The mode of passion and
3. The mode of ignorance.

The ones in the mode of goodness recommend the worship of Lord Vishnu, those in passion recommend the worship of Lord Brahma and those in ignorance recommend the worship of Lord Shiva.

Why is such a distinction made? All the people in this world are under the influence of three modes, which decide the levels of faith and intelligence they are born with. Each mode is characterized by a particular set of qualities and faults. Depending on which mode is binding an individual from his past life, he is attracted to a particular type of worship.

Shri Vyasa, an expert teacher, understood this and wanted to elevate each individual to the highest understanding. He concluded that just as we do not have the same book for all standards in an educational institution, it was not practical to have only one scripture for all. So, he compiled different scriptures and categorized them. This way, each person could start some sort of worship, even if it was not the highest form of worship. And if they remained sincere in their practice, they would gradually evolve and achieve the highest understanding as well.

Thus, if someone, based on his past faith, is attracted to the worship of a particular personality, a scripture will describe that personality as supreme to increase the person's faith in him. The hope is that the person will get connected to the Vedic path in some way and advance to spiritual realization, which is the ultimate goal of human life.

As far as the origin of Lord Shiva is concerned, depending on which Puranas one refers to, there are different descriptions. This is because, at least from the perspective of the seeker or worshipper, reality is state-specific. It's not that the Shiva Purana will describe Lord Vishnu as supreme, although Lord Vishnu is described as a very important person. The Shiva Purana will focus on describing Lord Shiva as the supreme. Why? Because that is the way the faith of the Lord Shiva worshippers will be enhanced. This also involves describing the origin in a particular way—the Shiva Purana will not explicitly talk about how Lord Shiva is subordinate to Lord Vishnu because that is how the faith of the worshipper is preserved.

Since all the information about spiritual subjects must come from the scriptures, the opinion of Sage Vyasa (who compiled all the Vedic literature) is to be considered the final word. He compiled the four Vedas, eighteen Puranas, 108 Upanishads and Vedanta Sutra (Vedanta means 'the conclusion or the end of all knowledge'). He also compiled the longest poem in the world—the Mahabharata. Still not satisfied, he also wrote the Bhagavat Purana, which he describes as the natural commentary on Vedanta Sutra.

Shrimad Bhagavat Purana is the conclusion of the message of all scriptures. Thus, logically, if we want to know how Lord Shiva originates, we should primarily focus on the Bhagavatam.

Also in this regard, the Skanda Purana mentions:

shiva-shastresu tad grahyam bhagavac-chastra-yogi yat
paramo vishnur evaikas taj jnanam moksha-sadhanam
shastranam nirnayas tv esas tad anyan mohanaya hi iti.

'Accept the verdict of the Shiva-Sastras
(like Shiva-Purana etc.) as long as it is in line and

accordance with the conclusions of Bhagavat-Sastras (Shrimad Bhagavatam) because there is only one Supreme, Lord Visnu, the knowledge of whom is the only means for liberation. This is the conclusion of all the revealed scriptures, and anything else other than this conclusion is meant only for the bewilderment of people in general.'

Thus, the information in this book is based on the conclusions of Shrimad Bhagavat Purana or the scriptures that support these conclusions.

Various scriptures like Shrimad Bhagavatam, Lord Brahma Samhita, Padma Purana, etc. explain the position of Lord Shiva in this universe:

1. Shrimad Bhagavatam (12.13.16) states *vaishnavanam yatha shambhu* i.e. Lord Shiva is the best of the Vaishnavas, the devotee of Lord Krishna.
2. Shrimad Bhagavatam (6.3.20) informs us that Lord Shiva is one of the twelve *Mahajanas*, the authorities on Vaisnava philosophy.
3. In Shrimad Bhagavatam (4.24.76), Lord Shiva states that if anyone reads his Rudra Gita prayer, he will invoke the mercy of the Supreme Lord, Krishna.
4. In Shrimad Bhagavatam (8.7.40), Lord Shiva tells his wife that he drank *Halahala*, the poison which came out during the churning of the ocean, to please Lord Vishnu. In the Padma Purana, Lord Shiva tells his wife Sati, '*sri rama rama rameti rame rame manorame sahasra namah tat tulyam rama nama varanane*'. He says that he relishes chanting the names of Lord Rama (an incarnation of Lord Krishna).

5. In Shrimad Bhagavatam (8.12.10), Lord Shiva gets bewildered when he sees the female form of Lord Vishnu, Mohini Murti. Lord Shiva later reveals that he is unable to completely understand the illusory energy of Lord Krishna.

6. In Bhagavad Gita (11.15), when Lord Krishna displays His Universal form, Arjuna says: 'My dear Lord Krishna, I see assembled in Your body, all the demigods and various other living entities. I see Lord Brahma sitting on the lotus flower, as well as Lord Shiva and all the sages and divine serpents.'

7. During Lord Krishna's pastimes (*lilas* or activities) in Vrindavan, Lord Shiva wants to participate in the *rasalila*[1] and desires to become a *gopi*.[2] Based on his wish, he receives the form of Gopishwar Mahadeva and resides in Vrindavan.

Furthermore, the Bhagavatam describes how Lord Shiva appears from Lord Brahma.

In the third canto of Srimad Bhagavatam, the process of creation is described. After Lord Brahma is born from the lotus sprouting from Lord Vishnu's navel, Lord Brahma becomes angry because his first four sons, the Kumaras, are not ready to obey his instruction to procreate and expand the population. Lord Brahma's anger comes out from his forehead, thus taking the form of Rudra or Lord Shiva. However, the fourth canto of the Bhagavatam describes how Lord Brahma prays to Lord Shiva to pacify him. Since

---

[1] Lord Krishna's dance with the gopis.

[2] Cowherd damsels.

Lord Brahma is the creator of the universe, to respect his role, Lord Shiva appears through him even though the latter is superior to the former. Lord Brahma is like one of us but with an immense amount of *punya*[3] to his credit, making him qualified for the post of Lord Brahma, whereas Lord Shiva is a different *tattva*[4] altogether and way beyond any ordinary or extraordinary living entity of the material world. Lord Brahma also has to die and give up his position when his lifespan is over but Lord Shiva is eternal.

One of the names of Lord Shiva is Vishwanath, which means the one who is the Lord of the universe. In contrast, Lord Vishnu or Lord Krishna is described as *anant koti brahmanda nayak*, meaning the master of unlimited universes.

In the Shrimad Bhagavatam, we also learn about the entire creation, which explains that Mahesh Dham (the abode of Lord Shiva) is located between Vaikuntha (the abode of Lord Vishnu) and Devi Dham (presided over by Goddess Durga), and this covers all material universes. Mahesh Dham is also eternal like Vaikuntha. But, if we have Lord Shiva who is born in this material universe through Lord Brahma, how can we have Lord Shiva's existence as above Devi Dham? This indicates that there are multiple manifestations of Lord Shiva. The Lord Shiva who exists above the Devi Dham is named Sadashiv. His abode, where he resides along with his followers to glorify and worship the Supreme Lord, is eternal. His followers glorify him, understanding that he is the glorious devotee of the Lord. But for all practical purposes,

---

[3] Piety.

[4] Category.

their primary object of glorification is the Supreme Lord, even though their glorification is done through Lord Shiva. So, they are Shaivite Vaishnavas.

Essentially, rather than creating conflict or having controversies, we have to understand that the Vedic path is inclusive, not exclusive i.e. it allows for multi-level worship and we encourage people to inquire about and understand the Vedic conclusion with an open mind. If someone is attracted to a particular devata, our goal should be to elevate people, not contradict and confuse them. Someone may be a Lord Shiva worshipper, so he quotes from the Shiva Purana. Someone else might be inclined to quote from the Vishnu Purana or the Bhagavat Purana and that is all right too. But sometimes, this gives rise to conflict and confusion, making people frustrated and turning them towards the path of materialism and atheism. If this happens, then we know that we have done a disservice to the person. Therefore, what is important is that we get a clear understanding based on scriptures, and then if we practice sincerely as per our capacity and pray for guidance about the absolute truth, things will become clearer and we will know how to best progress in our understanding of spiritual life.

Chapter 3

Shaivism vs Vaishnavism

One of the seemingly eternal, ongoing and senseless debates is Lord Shiva or Lord Krishna/Lord Vishnu: Who is the greatest?

Why do we always want things to be white or black? Because we are fanatics. Religion without proper philosophical understanding is nothing but sentimentalism or fanaticism. We need to remember that the Vedic path is an inclusive one, not an exclusive one. In order to accept someone, we do not need to reject the other. All can exist simultaneously. Our choices in life are influenced by what we have defined as our end goal.

Lord Krishna says in the Bhagavad Gita 9.25:

> *yanti deva-vrata devan*
> *pitrin yanti pitri-vratah*
> *chinty yanti bhutejya*
> *yanti mad-yajino 'pi mam*

'Those who worship the demigods will take birth
among the demigods; those who worship the ancestors
will go to the ancestors; those who worship ghosts
and spirits will take birth among such beings; and
those who worship Me will live with Me.'

This makes it clear that we get the results based on whom
we worship. Thus if someone is attached to Lord Shiva, he
will get Lord Shiva and attain his planet by becoming one
of his associates after leaving this world. And if someone
worships Lord Krishna, he will attain Lord Krishna in
His eternal abode called Goloka Vrindavan. So what is
the problem? Here, we are not even discussing who is the
greater of the two. Here we are discussing the hollowness
of this childish conflict.

If someone has made Lord Shiva the goal of his life, then
why not let him worship Lord Shiva? Let him go to Lord
Shiva and be happy. And if someone wants to worship Lord
Krishna, why not leave him alone with Lord Krishna? Why
do we need to stick our nose in someone's business? If we are
sincere in our mode of worship, we shall eventually reach
the highest platform of spiritual realization. Irrespective of
whoever is greater, to try to prove the superiority of 'our'
deity by demeaning the other is an absolute exhibition
of deep-rooted false ego and extreme fanaticism which
proclaims 'My way is the only way and it's the best.'

Actually speaking, when someone says, 'My deity is
the supreme', it sidelines the deity and puts their ego at
the forefront. 'Why is my deity the supreme?' 'Because
I worship him.' So the 'I' is the primary factor at play here.
The mentality is very clear. And if 'I' worship someone else,

then that deity becomes the supreme. So it is nothing but what satisfies our false ego and helps us maintain our false prestige through some deity. The deity in such cases simply becomes a medium to validate our thought patterns.

Lord Krishna recommends in the Bhagavad Gita that we should not discourage anyone from their particular mode of worship. Rather, we should keep doing our prescribed duty and following our mode of worship sincerely, and by our example, inspire everyone else towards perfection.

We must learn to appreciate and accept others as they are. The tendency to look down upon others and prove our superiority is a sign of false pride. This type of attitude does not get us anywhere in life. One could be superior, but trying to prove it to everyone so we can establish our supremacy is a sign of an acute mental ailment. We can always preach what we believe in and make people aware of the benefits of the same but then, we also have to let people decide for themselves. In the Bhagavad Gita, Lord Krishna speaks about various paths of Yoga and their ultimate benefits and limitations, but in the end, He tells Arjuna in Bhagavad Gita 18.63:

iti te jnanam akhyatam
guhyad guhya-taram maya
vimrishyaitad asheṣena
yathecchasi tatha kuru

'Thus, I have explained to you knowledge still more confidential. Deliberate on this fully, and then do what you wish to do.'

We see that Lord Krishna does not impose Himself. He lets Arjuna decide after deliberating on various choices. Lord Krishna appeals to Arjuna's intelligence rather than being attached to His 'perfect way'.

Wherever there is love, there is free will. And Lord Krishna has given everyone the free will to choose. And since we get the results according to the choices we make, we take their responsibility too. But that should not make us irresponsible or whimsical in our choices. All our choices should be based on scriptural evidence, since the scriptures are the guidebooks for humanity. The knowledge about personalities like Lord Shiva or Lord Krishna must come from scriptures and not from social media, movies, Google, TV serials or our misleading imagination. We must study the scriptures from proper, authentic teachers who are well versed in the intricacies of the subject matter and then based on that, decide our mode of worship.

In fact, just as Lord Shiva loves Lord Krishna and Lord Krishna loves Lord Shiva, we must learn to love and respect one another.

In Lord Shiva's own words from Shrimad Bhagavatam 4.24.28:

yah param ramhasah sakshat
tri-gunaj jiva-samjnitat
bhagavantam vasudevam
prapannah sa priyo hi me

'Any person who has surrendered to the Supreme Lord Vasudev (Krishna), the controller of

everything—material nature as well as the living
entity—is actually very dear to me.'

He further says, addressing the sons of King
Prachinbarhishat in the same chapter, 4.24.30:

> *atha bhagavata yuyam*
> *priyah stha achintya yatha*
> *na mad bhagavatanam cha*
> *preyan anyo 'sti karhichit*

'You are all devotees of the Lord, and as such
I appreciate that you are as respectable as the
Supreme Lord Himself. I know in this way that
the devotees also respect me and that I am dear
to them. Thus, no one can be as dear to the
devotees as I am.'

If we truly love the deities that we hold close to our hearts,
why can't we behave like Them? Are we not supposed to
learn from Their behaviour? What kind of followers are we
otherwise? A follower must follow the leader. But what are
we up to? Lord Shiva and Lord Krishna love each other, so
it is ironic that we are busy spreading hatred in the name
of religion.

In essence, we must leave one another alone and let
every individual worship their Lord. Those who wish to go
to Lord Shiva should be allowed to go to him and those who
hold Lord Krishna dear to their hearts should be allowed to
worship Him. Where is the room for interference if there is

no fanaticism on the part of the respective worshippers? In
order to grow in life, we need not pull someone else down.
That's a crab-like mentality. We can grow simply by focusing
on our growth.

Lord Shiva and Lord Krishna are simultaneously one
and different. They are one in the sense that they are the
manifestation of the same absolute truth but for different
functions and different characteristics controlling different
modes of nature.

For all practical purposes, at our level of devotion, if we
are not clear about who is the Supreme, the most important
thing is to not fight. Instead, embrace with sincerity whoever
the Supreme is according to our level of realization. We can
pray if we have some faith in Lord Vishnu/Lord Krishna
or Lord Shiva. Alternatively, we can pray to both of them,
'Please guide me. Please help me understand what is the
best way to serve You, what is the correct understanding.'
The Lord will reciprocate our sincerity and He will guide us
the same way He has guided many great souls of the past.

Chapter 4

The Identity of Lord Shiva

Lord Shiva is the Guru of the entire material creation. He is the master of material energy and the perfect example of what one should be.

The world needs a perfect teacher to guide everyone towards the right path. A perfect teacher does not just teach through his words but mainly by example. And who could be a better teacher than God Himself—the reservoir of all opulence including all knowledge? To be a perfect example, one needs to be perfect himself. And except the Supreme Lord, no one is perfect. Thus, to inspire the world and elevate the ones who have no hope at all, the Supreme Lord Krishna only transforms Himself into a special tattva called the Shiva tattva.

Lord Brahma, the first created being within the universe, substantiates this point in Brahma Samhita (5.45):

kshiram yatha dadhi vikara-vishesha-yogat
sanjayate na hi tatah prithag asti hetoh

yah shambhutam api tatha samupaiti karyad
govindam adi-purusham tam aham bhajami

'Just as milk is transformed into curd by the action
of acids, but yet the effect of curd is neither the
same as, nor different from, its cause, viz., milk,
so I adore the primaeval Lord Govinda, of whom
the state of Śambhu is a transformation for the
performance of the work of destruction.'

Lord Krishna does not deal with the material creation
directly in His original form as the matter is impure and
Lord Krishna is purity personified. Just like curd is nothing
but the transformed form of milk, Lord Shiva is none other
than Lord Krishna transformed when He comes in touch
with material creation. But just as milk and curd have
different properties, similarly, worship of Lord Krishna
and worship of Lord Shiva do not yield the same benefits.
Lord Krishna is like milk and Lord Shiva is the curd. From
milk, we can make specific preparations, while curd is used
to prepare some other specific preparations. Although they
are both manifestations of the same supreme person, we
must remember that they are in different roles. Just as in an
organization, no matter how big an individual is outside of
it, he only has powers limited to the role he plays within the
organization. Lord Shiva, similarly, has limitations in terms
of the position he holds within the universe or the role he
has to play. Those who worship Lord Krishna get some
benefits and those who worship Lord Shiva get different
benefits. Lord Krishna has sixty-four primary qualities,
Lord Vishnu has sixty, Lord Shiva has fifty-four and Lord

Brahma has forty-nine. There are many manifestations of Lord Shiva as there are countless universes, but there is only one Lord Krishna, the Supreme Lord (there cannot be many supremes). Thus, we must be wise enough to recognize and acknowledge the simultaneous oneness and differentiation of Lord Krishna and Lord Shiva and give them due respect without being sentimental about the subject.

The Shiva Tattva

Shiva tattva or the identity, function and position of Lord Shiva, is one of the most difficult spiritual truths to comprehend.

Confusion arises from the fact that Lord Shiva has different forms and abodes that are situated either in ignorance (the material world), pure goodness or complete transcendence (the spiritual realm). In addition to this, the individual names of these forms and abodes are interchangeable depending on the scriptural reference.

Both Lord Vishnu and Lord Shiva have a variety of forms and expansions within the spiritual and material realms. The easiest way to understand the Vishnu–Lord Shiva relationship is by accepting Lord Chaitanya Mahaprabhu's (none other than Lord Krishna who appeared 500 years ago as the avatar for Kaliyuga) philosophy of *achintya bheda adheda tattva*. This means that God, Bhagavan Shri Krishna, is inconceivably and simultaneously one with and different from His multifarious energies, including Lord Shiva.

Lord Shiva is considered the father of this universe and material nature while goddess Durga is considered the mother.

He is neither the Supreme Lord nor a *jiva-tattva* (an independent spirit soul, the category to which we belong).

Lord Shiva is the personal form through which the Supreme Lord works to inject the living entities (jiva-tattvas) into this material world.

Lord Shiva is in charge of the *tamo-guna*, the mode of ignorance, and is thus in the category of incarnations known as *gunavataras*.[5] From being simple-hearted to tricky, from being easily pleased to blazing with anger, Lord Shiva displays many facets of his personality, all in the service of his dear Lord Sri Krishna. He exhibits dependence on Lord Krishna and His devotees as well as surrenders and provides service to them.

Within the material universe, Lord Shiva holds almost all the powers of Lord Vishnu. His qualities are also above that of a living entity but he remains subservient to Lord Vishnu.

Source of Lord Shiva

The fifth canto of Shrimad Bhagavatam explains that the Supreme Lord Krishna expands into four forms known as the *chatur-vyuha*, comprising Vasudeva, Sankarshana, Pradyumna and Aniruddha.

From Lord Sankarshana, two personalities, Sadashiva and Maha-Vishnu arise.

---

[5] The avatars in charge of various *gunas* or modes. There are three gunavatars—mode of goodness (*sattvaguna*), mode of passion (*rajoguna*) and mode of ignorance (*tamoguna*).

This Sadashiva is the source of Lord Shiva/Rudra in the material creation for the purpose of destruction.

In other words, Shri Krishna in His form as Lord Sankarshana expands as Sadashiva. However, Sri Krishna alone is the supreme, origin and cause of all causes. In Gita (10.8), Sri Krishna emphatically proclaims this: 'I am the source of everything and everything emanates from Me, *aham sarvasya prabhavo, mattah sarvam pravartate.*'

Shrimad Bhagavatam (5.17.16) mentions:

bhavani-nathaiḥ stri-ganarbuda-sahasrair
avarudhyamano bhagavatash chatur-murter
maha-purushasya turiyam tamasim murtim
prakritim atmanah sankarshana-samjnam atma-
samadhi-rupena sannidhapyaitad abhigrinan
bhava upadhavati.

'In Ilavrita-Varsha, Lord Shiva is always encircled by 10 billion maidservants of Goddess Durga, who minister to him. The quadruple expansion of the Supreme Lord is composed of Vasudeva, Pradyumna, Aniruddha and Sankarshana. Sankarshana, the fourth expansion, is certainly transcendental, but because His activities of destruction in the material world are in the mode of ignorance, He is known as Tamasi, the Lord's form in the mode of ignorance. Lord Shiva knows that Sankarshana is the original cause of his own existence, and thus, he always meditates upon Him in trance by chanting the following mantra.'

Shrimad Bhagavatam (5.17.17–18):

om namo bhagavata maha-purushaya sarva-guna-
sankhyanayanantayavyaktaya nama iti.

'O Supreme Lord, I offer my respectful obeisances
unto You in Your expansion as Lord Saṅkarṣhaṇa.
You are the reservoir of all transcendental
qualities. Although You are unlimited, You
remain unmanifest to the non-devotees.'

bhaje bhajanyarana-pada-pankajam
bhagasya kritsnasya param parayanam
bhakteshv alam bhavita-bhuta-bhavanam
bhavapaham tva bhava-bhavam ishvaram

'O my Lord, You are the only worship-worthy
person, for You are the Supreme Lord, the
reservoir of all opulence. Your secure lotus feet are
the only source of protection for all Your devotees,
whom You satisfy by manifesting Yourself in
various forms. O, my Lord, You deliver Your
devotees from the clutches of material existence.
Non-devotees, however, remain entangled in
material existence by Your will. Kindly accept me
as Your eternal servant.'

In 5.17.22–23 Lord Shiva further prays:

yasyadya asid guna-vigraho mahan
vijnana-dhishnyo bhagavan ajah kila

yat-sambhavo 'ham tri-vrita sva-tejasa
vaikarikam tamasam aindriyam srije

ete vayam yasya vashe mahatmanah
sthitah shakunta iva sutra-yantritah
mahan aham vaikrita-tamasendriyah
srijama sarve yad-anugrahad idam

'From that Supreme Person appears Lord Brahma,
whose body is made from the total material
energy, the reservoir of intelligence predominated
by the passionate mode of material nature.
From Lord Brahma, I am born as a representation
of a false ego known as Rudra. By my power,
I create all the other demigods, the five elements
and the senses. Therefore, I worship the Supreme
Lord, who is greater than any of us and under
whose control are situated all the demigods,
material elements and senses,
and even Lord Brahma and I, are like birds
bound by a rope. Only by the Lord's grace can
we create, maintain and annihilate the material
world. Therefore, I offer my respectful obeisances
unto the Supreme Being.'

Thus, the original Lord Shiva, known as Sadashiva, originates
from Lord Sankarshana, who himself is an expansion of
Lord Krishna. This Sadashiva then incarnates as Lord Shiva
or Rudra into the material universes overseeing the realm of
ignorance and serving as the agent of destruction.

Oneness: Sadashiva is Narayana

According to Shri Baladeva Vidya Bhusana, a great Vaishnav *Acharya* of ancient times, Sadashiva is without a trace of mode of ignorance. He is the cause of all causes, and He is the Narayana form of *Svayam-Bhagavan*[6] Lord Krishna, the source of all other forms of Bhagavan. In the Taittiriya Upanishad, the names Narayana, Achyuta and Lord Shiva are used to indicate only one person.[7]

The Sadashiva mentioned in the Brahma Samhita is a vilasa expansion[8] of Lord Krishna, a form of Narayana.[9]

Sri Jiva Goswami, another great Vedic scholar mentions in his Paramatma Sandarbha 17: 'Brahma Samhita (5.8,10) says that Lord Sadashiva is a direct expansion of Lord Vishnu. However, the other Lord Shiva, manifest within the material universe known by different names such as Rudra, Shambhu etc., is not a direct expansion of Lord Vishnu.'

In Bhagavatamrita Kana, Shri Visvanatha Chakravarti Thakur, another prominent teacher in the Vedic line, says: 'Lord Sadashiva is transcendental to the three modes of material nature. He is the vilasa expansion of the Supreme Lord, Lord Vishnu. Sadashiva is also the source of the Lord Shiva serving as one of the gunavataras in the material creation. Thus, Sadashiva is equal to Lord Vishnu, superior

---

[6] The source of all other forms of Bhagavan.

[7] Laghu Bhagavatamrita, I.2.31.

[8] Vilasa expansions are the expanded forms of God endowed with different degrees of powers from the original Godhead, Bhagavan Sri Lord Krishna.

[9] Laghu Bhagavatamrita, I.5.298.

to Lord Brahma and superior to and separate from the conditioned, living entities like us.'

Srila Prabhupada (founder Acharya of ISKCON) further clarifies: 'In the Vayu Purana, there is a description of Sadashiva in one of the Vaikuntha planets. That Sadashiva is a direct expansion of Lord Krishna's form for the sake of pastimes. It is said that Lord Shambhu [Lord Shiva in the material universes] is an expansion from the Sadashiva in the Vaikuntha planets [Lord Vishnu]' (Chaitanya Charitamrita. 1.6.79)

Thus, when the material modes come into contact with Lord Vishnu, by his own sweet will, He takes on the quality of a demigod and also associates with the modes as Lord Shiva. Although ultimately, He is the controller of the modes of material nature, He willingly accepts that contact and influence. In each material universe, this manifestation of Lord Shiva as the demigod overseeing the mode of ignorance is not eternal.

The Abode of Sadashiva

Sadashiva's abode is called Sadashiva Loka, and it is situated above the material universe, slightly below Goloka, Lord Krishna's planet. It is eternal, spiritual, inexhaustible, full of eternal happiness and devoid of any disease.

Shri Sanatana Goswami, a prominent acharya on the Vedic teachings, mentions in the great scripture called Brihad Bhagavatamrita (1.2.96): 'The abode of Lord Shiva lies outside the material universe and all its seven coverings.'

Shri Rupa Goswami, another great teacher in the line of Lord Chaitanya describes in his Laghu Bhagavatamrita

(1.5.298): 'Shiva's abode is manifest in the northeast part of Vaikunthaloka. Sadashiva Loka is attained by the best of Lord Shiva's devotees who know that Lord Shiva is nondifferent from Sri Krishna and not by others.'

The Geographical Location

After passing through the eight material coverings, and after crossing the Viraja (the river that divides the material world and the spiritual world) and the planet of Lord Brahma (the highest material planet), one comes to the planet of Lord Shiva called Shiva Dham. One portion of this is called Mahakal Dham, and is enveloped in darkness; interpenetrating this portion of Shiva Dham, where shines the Sadashivaloka, full of great light. This Shiva Dham is situated on the boundary of material and spiritual worlds, three-fourths of it lying in the spiritual realm and one-fourth lying in the material realm. Here, Lord Shiva resides in his eternal form of Sadashiva.

Chapter 5

The Birth of Lord Shiva

The third canto of Shrimad Bhagavatam describes how Lord Shiva appears as the gunavatar within this world. At the beginning of creation, the Supreme Lord *Garbhodakshayi*[10] Lord Vishnu decides to create this cosmic manifestation to facilitate the independent desires of the living entities who have gone astray from His loving service. He lies in the causal ocean (an ocean existing as a boundary between the material and spiritual realm), and by His sweet will, a lotus flower grows from His navel. Upon that lotus flower, Lord Brahma is born. Lord Brahma, not knowing what is to be done and what is not to be done, is in a bewildered condition. Seeing his eagerness to know the purpose for which he was born, the Supreme Lord from within his heart instructs him to perform *tapa* (austerities). Through his austerities, Lord Brahma is empowered by Lord Narayana with all of the faculties required to create everything within this cosmic creation.

---

[10] The one who lies down in the womb of the universe.

During the process of creation, the four Kumaras, the eldest sons of Lord Brahma, emerge from his mind. Being his original sons, he instructs them to procreate and produce offspring to help in the creation process. But the four Kumaras, being incredibly intelligent and having been born from the mind of Lord Brahma himself, have no desire to have wives or children, or engage in this family business of producing offspring. So they deny the request.

Lord Brahma becomes very angry at his sons for their disobedience. At the same time, he understands that they are spiritually advanced and are denying his request because they have a higher goal in mind. Even though the thought that they are disobeying his instructions makes him angry, he does not manifest his anger and keeps it within himself. Anger is born from a mixture of passion and ignorance.

From the great stirring of passion and ignorance within the heart of Lord Brahma, a powerful energy is released from between his two eyebrows. And from that, a beautiful young child is born, whose colour is blue and red. Blue is the colour of tamoguna (mode of ignorance) and red is the colour of rajoguna (mode of passion). As soon the child is born, he begins to ask, 'My dear father, where should I go and what should I do?' Because he is crying, he is named Rudra by Lord Brahma. Rudra means 'the one who is crying'. Lord Brahma instructs this son, on behalf of the Supreme Lord, to predominate over the mode of ignorance. Since the entire material existence is essentially in the mode of ignorance, Lord Rudra is the predominating deity of the entire material creation. He is also known as Shankar, which means he is the support of the entire creation, the entire universe. Lord Shankar is none other than a plenary portion (distinct yet equally powerful form) of the Supreme Lord Krishna

Himself. He is utterly pure, He is Godhead and the master of all souls. But the Supreme Lord, for the sake of incarnating in these gunavatars, accepts the influence of rajoguna and tamoguna upon Himself just for the purpose of engaging in this very important, essential universal function. Therefore, Lord Shiva is none other than Lord Krishna or Narayana, who, by His own sweet will, accepts the subordination and influence of tamoguna. And because He is accepting this position, He is considered to be the most merciful of all personalities.

After Shankar is born, Lord Brahma explains to him, 'Now, my other four sons, the Kumaras, will not procreate. So now, you produce offspring.' Shankar begins to produce offspring in exceedingly large quantities. But all his offspring are very prominently in the mode of passion or ignorance and therefore are incredibly fiery, angry personalities marching through every corner of the universe and causing tremendous havoc. Regardless, he continues to create till finally, Lord Brahma has to tell him, 'My dear son, please let me do the creation. You go into the forest. There is a mountain. You go on that mountain in the forest and sit in peaceful meditation until I call upon you at the time of destruction. You simply go and meditate on the beautiful form of our master, the Supreme Lord Narayana.' Upon receiving these instructions, Lord Shiva, giving up his position as a creator, begins to perform penances and sit in the sublime state of *samadhi*,[11] fixing his mind and consciousness on the divine form of the Supreme Lord. That is why the most common picture of Lord Shiva that we see is when he is sitting in the lotus posture, in this peaceful state of divine meditation.

---

[11] A deep state of meditation.

Chapter 6

Goddess Parvati: The Universal Mother

Mother Parvati is the eternal consort and *shakti* (strength) of Lord Shiva. She is the mother of the Universe in her role as Annapurna. Just as Lord Shiva is the master of the material universe, she, in her form as Durga, is the controller of the material creation. She carries out various responsibilities within the material realm, which assist the Supreme Lord in the purpose of creation, maintenance and destruction in various capacities.

However, most popularly, she is the *mahamaya*[12] shakti of the Supreme Lord. In this role, she keeps the living entities under illusion and also inflicts threefold miseries on them.

One might wonder why she would do that. She is a mother after all, and for a mother, no matter how fallen the children are, she is always forgiving and wishes the best for them. Well, the reason is quite interesting.

---

[12] The illusory energy.

This material world is known as *Durg* (fort) and because she is the controller in charge, she is known as Durga. In essence, she is the jailer of the material world and being so, she has a thankless task.

A jailer, being the servant of the government, punishes the criminals not out of enmity, but with the motive of rectifying their wrong mentality. The prisoners are subjected to suffering till they cooperate with the laws of the government. As soon as they show good behaviour, their sentence gets reduced and they may be freed much earlier. In the entire process, the jailer is simply carrying out his duty.

Similarly, when Mother Durga inflicts the threefold miseries—Adhyatmika Klesha: miseries caused by mind and body, Adhibhautik Klesha: miseries caused by other beings and Adhidaivik Klesha: miseries caused by natural calamities—upon the living entities, she does so only on those who have rebelled against the laws of God. These miseries are meant to act as an impetus for everyone to want to leave this world of misery, as described by the Supreme Lord Krishna in the Bhagavad Gita (8.15). When a person suffers, he might develop a desire to not repeat his mistakes and thus, begin to lead a righteous life in accordance with God's laws to avoid any future suffering. When Durga Devi sees that a person has now turned to God, she considers her job accomplished and feels happy.

So this is a thankless task she does for Lord Krishna to rectify the souls' wrong mentality. As spirit soul and spiritual beings, we all are part of God and are therefore meant to always be engaged in His service and enjoy His association.

To cooperate with the will of God is our eternal, natural position and when we try to live a life independent of Him, we immediately come under the control of Mahamaya and have to come to this world of misery, just as a citizen comes under the control of the law enforcement agencies if he tries to act independent of the government.

Through her role as Durga, Mother Parvati is motivating us to return to where we belong, which is the spiritual realm where we can be eternally happy. Thus, her being Mahamaya, the illusory potency of the Supreme Lord, is an act of great compassion. Isn't this exactly how a mother would behave towards a naughty child? She would have to be strict with her child to correct him, just to ensure that he does not get into any more trouble. Hence, whenever we go through any miseries in life, the immediate reason could be anything, but the ultimate reason is that we have turned away from God and the law of karma now controls us. And by Durga Devi's mercy, if we turn to Him again by engaging in His devotional service, we will be saved too. So when problems pop up in life, instead of trying to take care of the symptoms, understand the root cause: karma, which is due to disobedience of God's laws and living a whimsical life rooted in false ego. Therefore, to save ourselves in such situations, we must intensify our devotional service to Lord Krishna rather than becoming complacent.

However, as previously noted, being a mother, Parvati was unwilling to serve as the means of causing suffering to living beings. Thus, at one point in history, feeling extremely dejected, she went to the holy land called

Mayapur, on the banks of Ganga, to perform austerities to please Lord Krishna. When the Lord appeared, she pleaded and revealed her state of mind.

She said, 'My dear Lord, everyone is serving you by trying to bring people close to you, but I have this thankless task of keeping souls in illusion and away from you. I even have to punish them. I am not happy. I also wish to directly participate in your pastimes of compassion.'

Hearing her desire, the Supreme Lord manifested a most enchanting form with a golden complexion, hands raised and chanting the holy names:

Hare Krishna Hare Krishna, Krishna Krishna Hare Hare
Hare Ram Hare Ram, Ram Ram Hare Hare

Then the merciful Lord assured Parvati, 'Dear Goddess, please do not worry anymore. Your desire will certainly be fulfilled when I appear in Kaliyuga in this glorious form in this holy land. At that time, you will reside here with Lord Shiva. You will be worshipped as "Praudh" Maya and Lord Shiva will be famous as "Vriddha" Lord Shiva. In that pastime, both of you will guide everyone in my devotional service [bhakti] along with protecting my dham.'

Mother Parvati was overjoyed and she took the dust of the Lord's lotus feet on her head and applied it in the middle part of her hair which is also known as simanta. Since then, that place has become famous as 'Simanta Dweep', where devotees can still go and relish its beauty. A temple has been constructed there, and beautiful deities of Parvati and Lord Chaitanya have been installed by devotees.

Thus, Mother Parvati is one of the most important personalities in the pastimes of the Supreme Lord, always working towards bringing the lost souls back to Him, sometimes by the blessing of punishment and sometimes by directly guiding them in devotional service to the Lord.

Understanding her true inner mood, we must always pray to her to guide us towards Lord Krishna, just as the Gopis prayed to her for Lord Krishna's association.[13]

---

[13] The gopis, out of their pure devotion, always wanted to be with Lord Krishna and engage in His devotional service of love. Thus, they had prayed to Goddess Katyayani (a form of Goddess Parvati).

Chapter 7

The Birth of Kartikeya:
The Mighty Commander

After severe austerities, Tarakasur, the mighty demon, received immense powers from Lord Brahma. He wished to be immortal but Lord Brahma flatly refused. He said that since he himself was not immortal, he was incapable of giving this boon. Tarakasur was desperate. So, he asked for a benediction that if he should die at all, he could only be killed by the son of Lord Shiva. Tarakasur was certain that this would never happen, since Lord Shiva was always absorbed in deep meditation and thus, was not interested in anything else. True to his nature, after receiving these powers, he went on a rampage, wreaked havoc in the three worlds by destroying the followers of Vedic dharma and even defeated the celestial Gods.

Seeing no other alternative, all the heavenly Gods, headed by Lord Indra, approached Lord Brahma for help, who in turn, took them to Lord Shiva at Kailash.

Lord Shiva is extremely compassionate and cannot see anyone in distress. Seeing the powerful caretakers of the universe at his doorstep in a helpless condition, he asked them to reveal their minds. Lord Brahma, without wasting any time, spoke of the atrocities of Tarakasur. The celestial gods, living in constant fear, were unable to discharge their respective duties allocated to them by the Supreme Lord, and as a result, the universe was in chaos. The only solution was for a powerful son to be born of Lord Shiva, who would then destroy the demon as per the terms of the benediction.

The son represents the partial portion or power of the father. Lord Shiva, hearing their desperate plea, agreed to help his divine visitors, but expressed apprehension as to who would be able to handle or absorb his plenary power. Saying this, Lord Shiva released a portion of his power onto the ground. Lord Brahma and others requested the powerful fire god, Agni, to absorb it. Agni did as asked. But a problem arose. Mother Parvati arrived on the scene and when she saw what Agni had done, she took offence. 'How dare you engage in such impudence? When did you become so powerful that you began thinking you were competent enough to hold my husband's power in your body?'

'Since you have performed this horrible act, I curse you. From now on, you will become an all-devourer. Whatever and whoever comes in touch with you will be destroyed. And you will also continue to be scorched and thus suffer the heat of this power.' Saying this, she angrily left the scene, and so did Lord Shiva.

Meanwhile, the celestial gods performed some *yajnas*[14] and offered oblations[15] into the fire. When they partook of

---

[14] Vedic fire ceremonies.

[15] Things offered to the deity in a yajna.

the remnants of what was offered into the fire, the portions of Lord Shiva's power from Agni also got transferred into their bodies. This resulted in a constant burning sensation in their bodies as well, leading to immense suffering. They were already troubled by Tarakasur, and now with this heat, a new problem had arisen. When they approached Lord Shiva again, he suggested they do *vaman*[16] to get the power out. The celestial gods did as instructed and instantly felt relieved. However, Agni continued to suffer from the heat and upon the advice of Lord Brahma, he approached Lord Shiva for help. Out of kindness, Lord Shiva candidly explained to him that his suffering was a result of him mistakenly thinking that he was qualified enough to absorb Lord Shiva's mighty power in his body.

The merciful Lord then forgave Agni and also revealed to him the way out. Lord Shiva said, 'Dear Agni! You should place this power in the body of some woman. This way, you will be relieved from your misery.'

Agni felt apprehensive and told the Lord that it was impossible since no one could hold his power. Right then, the great sage Narada arrived and told Agni to do as guided. Narada told him to place this power in the first woman to come and take a bath at the holy *Prayag*[17] in the cold winter month of Magh. As per the will of providence, the wives of the *saptarishis*[18] reached Prayag in the early morning hours

---

[16] A ayurvedic way of cleansing the body by inducing vomit.

[17] The confluence of the three sacred rivers: Ganga, Yamuna and Saraswati.

[18] Seven great sages: Vashishtha, Kashyap, Gautama, Atri, Vishwamitra, Bhrigu and Bharadvaj.

(*Brahma Muhurat*). After bathing, since they felt cold, six of them sat next to a fire for some warmth. It was then that the power of Lord Shiva from Agni entered their bodies through their pores. Finally, Agni felt relieved.

As time passed, these six saintly ladies became pregnant (due to holding Lord Shiva's power in their bodies) and not understanding the cause, their husbands rejected them. Feeling morose, all six of them went to the Himalayas to perform austerities. There, in due course, they separately gave birth to various limbs of a child, but the mountain on which they resided could not bear the weight of these powerful limbs and dropped them in the holy Ganga.

Being a mother, Ganga united all these limbs, and thus, a powerful child came into being. However, the Ganga could not bear the radiance of this child, so she left him in a forest close by.

As soon as the child took birth, there were celebrations in the heavens, and celestial music was played and heard everywhere. The entire forest seemed to have lit up due to the effulgence of the child.

As he lay in the forest, by divine will, the great sage Vishwamitra arrived there. When the sage saw the child, he knew immediately that he was not ordinary. He offered beautiful prayers in the glorification of the child. To the sage's surprise, the child spoke and requested him to perform his birth and naming ceremony. Vishwamitra happily consented. He performed the Vedic ceremony that is usually performed at birth and named the child Kartikeya. In return as remuneration, the child gave transcendental knowledge to the sage.

Lord Brahma also arrived and took the newborn on his lap, kissed him out of affection and blessed him with immense powers and invincible weapons. Receiving these benedictions, the child immediately got up and climbed the nearby mountains and started destroying the peaks. When the demons who lived there came charging in to attack him, he chased them away. But this battle was so ghastly that the three worlds started trembling. Carefully analysing the situation and considering the child to be the cause of the disturbance, Lord Indra came and angrily attacked him. However, the blow by Indra produced a *skanda*[19] from the body of Kartikeya. As Indra attacked, one after the other, four such skandas manifested and simultaneously attacked the king of heaven. Indra fled the battlefield and hid in a secret place. The child gave chase and reached the heavens looking for him. As he was searching the celestial realm, he was suddenly noticed by six heavenly girls known as *kritikas,* who instantly developed motherly affection for him. The girls came running, picked him up and showered him with love. Each of them argued, wanting to feed him, and just to reciprocate their affection, the child took six different forms and drank their milk, therefore giving them immense joy. Finally, they brought him to their planet and began to take care of him as their child.

After much time had passed, Mother Parvati curiously asked about the whereabouts of the power that Lord Shiva had released. Lord Shiva immediately summoned all the celestial Gods and asked them as to what had happened with his power. When he and Mother Parvati came to know

---

[19] A powerful warrior.

that a powerful child had manifested from the power and was now under the loving care of the kritikas, both became eager to see their son. Lord Shiva summoned Nandi, his carrier, and other *ganas*,[20] and asked them to go and bring Kartikeya to Kailash.

When Lord Shiva's army reached the abode of the kritikas, the girls became afraid and spoke to Kartikeya about their safety. Kartikeya assured them that as long as he was there, no one could even enter the house or harm them. He comforted them by saying, 'Dear Mothers! Please do not be afraid. I am quite capable of defeating everyone. Please do not consider me a mere child.'

As they were conversing, however, Nandi came forward and expressed that they had simply come to take Kartikeya back to Kailash, and had no intention of fighting at all. Nandi requested, 'Dear Kartikeya! Everyone, including Lord Brahma, along with your parents, Lord Shiva and Mother Parvati, are eagerly waiting for you at Kailash. Perhaps, you are not aware of the purpose of your birth. You are born to kill Tarakasur. Please come with us and fulfil your mission of relieving the heavens of the panic that Tarakasur has caused.'

Kartikeya happily agreed and asked for permission from his caretaking mothers. The kritikas were devastated and cried as they hugged Kartikeya. Giving them the knowledge of self-realization, Kartikeya pacified them to some extent. With a very heavy heart, the kritikas finally consented and cried as Kartikeya departed.

---

[20] Associates.

As they reached Kailash, Lord Shiva and Mother Parvati, along with their remaining associates, eagerly rushed to the spot to see their beloved child. Everyone was in bliss and Lord Shiva's associates, in particular, danced their way to see Kartikeya. When they met, Mother Parvati showered immense affection on the child and Lord Shiva bathed him with sacred ingredients. All the celestial Gods arrived, and each one present at the scene blessed Kartikeya with a long life and innumerable gifts, dazzling ornaments, powerful weapons and immense powers.

Kartikeya's fame had already spread far and wide. Finally, the celestial gods requested Lord Shiva to allow Kartikeya to lead them and kill Tarakasur, the mission he was born to accomplish. A fierce battle took place. The three worlds trembled and there was great destruction on both sides. Eventually, as was destined, the invincible Kartikeya destroyed Tarakasur, giving joy to the hearts of all. That which was practically impossible even for the powerful rulers of the universe was easily achieved by him, being the son of the great destroyer of all the worlds, Lord Shiva.

Chapter 8

The Birth of Lord Ganesh
(From the Brahma Vaivarta Purana)

Lord Brahma describes Lord Ganesh's identity in the Brahma Samhita (5.50):

> *yat-pada-pallava-yugam vinidhaya kumbha-*
> *dvandve pranama-samaye sa ganadhirajah*
> *vighnan vihantum alam asya jagat-trayasya*
> *govindam adi-purusham tam aham bhajami*

'I adore the primaeval Lord Govinda, whose lotus feet are always held by Lord Ganesh upon the pair of tumuli protruding from his elephant head in order to obtain power for his function of destroying all the obstacles on the path of progress of the three worlds.'

Lord Ganesh occupies a prominent position within the universe. He is the recipient of the first worship in any Vedic ceremony. Most people worship him as the remover of obstacles. However, a less-known fact about him is that he not only removes obstacles from the path of pious souls, but he also puts obstacles on the path of impious souls. When Lord Krishna/Lord Vishnu incarnates in this world, Lord Ganesh also descends in some capacity to assist the Lord in His mission to re-establish *dharma* (religious principles). When Lord Krishna was in Dwarka, Lord Ganesh appeared as one of his sons named Charudeshna.

In fact, when the great Sage Vyasa was compiling the Vedic literature for the benefit and guidance of entire humanity, in order to bring the common masses to the path of morality and ultimately devotional service to Lord Krishna, he contemplated the great epic Mahabharata. However, he was faced with a big problem. The Mahabharata was going to be his longest compilation and he had already taken a long time to write other scriptures. Since he could not afford to delay the compilation, he decided the best way would be to dictate it to someone else and have it written. This way, things would get done faster. Vyasa needed the perfect scribe and after much thought, he concluded that the person best suited for the job was none other than Lord Ganesh. When approached, Lord Ganesh happily consented and thus the monumental Mahabharata, the longest poem/compilation in the world with 1,10,000 verses, was completed.

Thus, Lord Ganesh, being Lord Shiva's son, is special. There are various stories about his birth, but here we focus on the little-known account from the Brahma Vaivarta Purana.

This description of the appearance of Lord Ganesha is given in Ganapati *khanda*[21] of Brahma Vaivarta Purana. The popular story of how Mother Parvati created Lord Ganesha from her cosmetics is given in Rudra Samhita, Kumara khanda of the Shiva Purana. Lord Brahma confirms the version presented below. The different versions mentioned in the Puranas are due to the variation in pastimes that took place in different yugas.

Sage Narada Muni inquired from Lord Narayana about Lord Ganesha's birth and his qualities.

Lord Narayana explained that, after the birth of Kartikeya, the commander-in-chief of the demigods, Mother Parvati requested Lord Shiva for one more son. At the request of his beloved wife, Mahadeva asked her to perform a ceremony called *punyaka vrata* to Lord Krishna. The procedures include singing kirtans and offering *bhoga*,[22] flower garlands as well as tulsi lamps to Lord Hari.

After explaining the details, Lord Shiva, who can award the fruit of penances, went to perform meditation on Lord Hari.

Following the order of Lord Shiva, Mother Parvati arranged for all the paraphernalia required to be used in the ceremony, with Sanat-kumara, the head priest. On the first day of the year-long observance, everyone arrived on Mount Kailash to greet and offer their blessings to Mother Parvati for the successful completion of the ceremony. The host, Lord Shiva, made comfortable arrangements for the guests.

---

[21] A section of the scripture.

[22] Offerings of purely-cooked, delicious food items.

After satisfying the guests, Lord Shiva requested Lord Vishnu to sit on the elevated throne and inquired: 'O all cognizant Lord Srinivasa, kindly instruct us on the performance of this ceremony.' Smiling gently, Lord Vishnu replied: 'O master of Parvati, the essence of performing any activity or any ceremony is devotion to Lord Sri Krishna, which is very rare. It is through His devotees' mercy that one can get devotion to Him. A devotee becomes qualitatively equal to the Lord. He never perishes even after the annihilation of this world and returns to the Lord's abode, Goloka Vrindavana. O Shiva, you devastate the whole world, but you cannot harm My devotee, nor does any powerful illusory energy delude them because of My mercy upon them.'

'Your wife is the mother of all living entities in this material world. By the influence of this ceremony, Parvati will beget the child who will be the partial representative of Lord Krishna. He will be known as Lord Ganesha (master of all *devaganas*),[23] Vighnanighan (remover of obstacles), Lambodara (whose belly is stretched out due to offerings made in ceremony), Gajanana (elephant-faced) and Ekadanta (one who has only one tooth). And by My blessing, he will receive the first worship in any auspicious occasion.'

After completion of the punyaka vrata, Sanat-kumara requested Mother Parvati to give him Lord Shiva as his remuneration. On hearing this demand, Mother Parvati fell unconscious. When brought back to consciousness, she said, 'Just like the worship of a tree is useless without worship to Mother Earth, who is the cause of the tree,

---

[23] The celestial gods.

similarly, what is the use of any benediction to me, if my
husband is taken away from me?'

While this negotiation was going on, Lord Narayana
descended from the sky. His beautiful form was seen by
everyone assembled. The Lord cannot be seen by anyone
who does not have devotion to Him, even after millions
of births. He told Mother Parvati that, for the completion
of the ceremony and to obtain the result of it, she should
fulfil the desire of sage Sanat-kumara. She should give him
Lord Shiva in charity, but then exchange her husband with
the offering of a cow to the sage. Mother Parvati did as
instructed and her husband was returned.

Lord Krishna Appears

At that moment, a radiant sphere of light appeared,
surpassing the brilliance of millions of suns. It was Lord
Krishna, and all the present demigods praised His radiance.
After Mother Parvati's prayers, Lord Krishna became
pleased with her and revealed to her His charming, eternal,
youthful form, holding a flute, decorated with a forest
flower garland, peacock feather on his head, yellowish
garments and an enchanting smiling face. His beauty
defeated the beauty of millions of cupids.[24] Seeing this form,
Mother Parvati desired a son like Him. Understanding her
wish, the Lord instantly granted her wish and disappeared
soon after.

Mother Parvati then distributed an immense charity,
after which she and Lord Shiva spent time together at

---

[24] Cupid is the most beautiful god of love, Kamadev.

their residence. When they were engaged in a union, a brahman knocked on their door while desperately calling out for food. His body was emaciated by penances, and he was very hungry. Both Lord Shiva and Parvati received the untimely guest. The brahman explained his condition and asked for food that had been prepared for the punyaka ceremony. Lord Shiva and Mother Parvati went to bring the food, but the brahmana suddenly disappeared. Shocked, they lamented for not being able to serve him. At that time, a divine voice spoke from the sky, 'O Parvati. Do not lament. Go inside your residence and see the newborn child that has appeared there. The brahman was none other than Lord Vishnu.'

Parvati rushed inside and to her amazement, a beautiful child had appeared on the bed. Delighted, her heart experienced a profound joy, akin to that of a poverty-stricken person who discovers a big treasure house, or that of those enduring drought when rain finally arrives. She called for Lord Shiva to see the child and both of them heartily embraced the child.

Sanideva's Arrival

Hearing the news of the arrival of a newborn baby in the home of Lord Shiva, all the sages, demigods and other celestial beings expert in music and dance, such as the *gandharvas* and *kinnaras,* arrived at their residence to see the child, and offered their blessings upon him. Lord Shiva also distributed charity to the brahmans.

Amongst them was the son of the sun god, Sanideva. As he arrived, he offered his obeisances to Lord Vishnu,

Lord Brahma, Lord Shiva, Suryadeva and Yamaraja, and
asked permission to see the child. His face was gently
bowed down, his eyes were half-closed in meditation, his
mind was fixed on Lord Krishna, and he was remembering
Lord Krishna internally and externally. He went into the
chambers where Mother Parvati was sitting with her child,
Lord Ganesha, but did not glance at them. Mother Parvati
asked him, 'What is the matter? Why have you lowered
your head instead of seeing the newborn child?'

Sanideva replied:

Everyone in this world suffers the reactions of his own
activity (karma) by either enjoying or suffering. These
activities decide one's birth as the king of demigods,
Indra, or an insignificant insect. One gets a beautiful
attractive body or an ugly one based on his activities
performed. Since my childhood, I was a devotee of Lord
Krishna and was always engaged in his meditation.
Once, my wife desired to have union with me while
I was in meditation on the Lord's lotus feet. Being
oblivious to my surroundings, I could not respond to
her desire and she cursed me, saying that whomever
I glanced at would be thus destroyed. To avoid violence,
now I don't glance at anyone.

Mother Parvati remembered Lord Hari. 'Everyone is
controlled by the Lord's desire,' she replied and asked
Sanideva to look at her and her son. Confused, Sanideva
hesitated. Avoiding the mother, he only glanced at the child
from the corner of his left eye. At once, the child's head got
separated from his trunk and went back to Goloka, where

it merged into Lord Krishna. As Mother Parvati saw her dead son, she fell unconscious. Everyone stood stunned, including Lord Shiva.

Seeing this condition, Lord Hari went to the northern side of the bank of the River Puspabhadra where an elephant was resting in the forest facing north. The Lord immediately cut off its head with the Sudarsana chakra[25] and brought it back to Mount Kailash. He placed that head on the trunk of the dead child and revived his consciousness.

Seeing the child alive, the whole atmosphere filled with joy and bliss. In this way, the child became known as Gajanana.

---

[25] The ultimate disc weapon of the Lord.

Chapter 9

Kailash

Mount Kailash, 22,000 feet (6705 metres) above sea level, is a special and sacred dham because it is there that Lord Shiva meditates deeply on Lord Krishna and meets with great sages like Narada. It was at Mount Kailash that the Ganga River descended with great force from the spiritual world to the material world and was caught by Lord Shiva in his matted locks.

Kailash is also known as Mount Meru, the centre of the universe. Throughout the ages, it has been called by various names, including Jewel Peak, Lotus Mountain and Silver Mountain. The city of Kuvera, the treasurer of the demigods, is said to be near Mount Kailash.

Local Buddhists recognize the spiritual significance of the mountain and consider it one of their holiest places of pilgrimage. It is also fervently worshipped by followers of the Bon religion, the religion of Tibet before the arrival of Buddhism in the seventh century. Tibetans say that there is an invisible ladder connecting Kailash to heaven, while the rulers of ancient Tibet were said to have descended to Kailash from heaven attached to the ropes of light by their citizens.

People across the world have attempted to climb it but all their efforts have been in vain. No one has ever been successful. Reinhold Messner, the famous Austrian mountaineer who has scaled all fourteen of the 8,000-metre mountains of the world, was offered a license to climb Mount Kailash by the Chinese government in the 1980s. He declined, saying, 'If we conquer this mountain, then we conquer something in people's souls.'[26]

Through the centuries, Westerners have been attracted to visit Kailash, not for spiritual reasons but out of curiosity. The first recorded Westerner to visit Kailash was an Italian Jesuit missionary, Ippolito Desideri, in 1715. He wrote:

> Kailash is a mountain of excessive height and great circumference, always enveloped in clouds, covered in snow and ice, and most horrible, barren, steep and cold. The Tibetans walk devoutly around the base of this mountain, which takes several days, and they believe this will bring them great indulgences. Owing to the snow on the mountain, my eyes became so inflamed that I nearly lost my sight.[27]

[26] Daniel Brett, 'Mount Kailash: The Sacred Himalayan Peak Forbidden To Climbers', Noble Sapien, 2 March 2022, https://noblesapien.com/soul/mount-kailash-the-sacred-himalayan-peak-forbidden-to-climbers/.

[27] Filippo De Filippi, ed., An Account of Tibet: The Travels of Ippolito Desideri of Pistoia, S.J. (1712–1727) (India: Routledge, 2004).

When we visit Mount Kailash, we pass by the sacred Mansarovar lake.

On the top of the sacred Mount, Lord Shiva and Mother Parvati once sat in deep meditation on Lord Krishna for twelve years by the calculation of the demigods. No rain fell in the area during that period, so Lord Shiva called Lord Brahma to create a sacred lake where he and his consort could bathe. Lord Brahma then created Mansarovar from his mind. After their bath, a self-manifested, golden *shivaling*[28] appeared in the centre of the lake.

The Real Kailash

When we, the fallible, imperfect creatures of this world, think of Kailash, we think of an invincible and mysterious snow-capped mountain. However, that is just the external covering of the original beauty and glory of Kailash for those who are not qualified or advanced in spiritual vision yet. Until we become qualified to see through our eyes that which is beyond our vision, we must learn to see it through our ears i.e. hearing. The Shrimad Bhagavatam, fourth canto, chapter 6, text 28–41 gives a beautiful description of the abode of Lord Shiva as the celestial gods visit it to appease him:

> The abode known as Kailash is full of different herbs and vegetables, and it is sanctified by Vedic hymns and mystic yoga practice. Thus the residents of that abode are demigods by birth and have all mystic powers. Besides them, there are other human beings, who are known as

---

[28] A symbol of Lord Shiva.

Kinnaras and Gandharvas and are accompanied by their beautiful wives, who are known as Apsaras, or angels.

Kailash is full of mountains filled with all kinds of valuable jewels and minerals and surrounded by all varieties of valuable trees and plants. The top of the hill is well populated by various types of deer.

There are many waterfalls, and in the mountains, there are many beautiful caves in which the very beautiful wives of the mystics are found.

On Kailash Hill, there is always the rhythmical sound of the peacocks' sweet vibrations and the bees' humming. Cuckoos are always singing, and other birds whisper amongst themselves.

There are tall trees with straight branches that appear to call the sweet birds, and when herds of elephants pass through the hills, it appears that the Kailash Hill moves with them. When the waterfalls resound, it appears that Kailash Hill does too.

The whole of Kailash Hill is decorated with various kinds of trees, of which the following names may be mentioned: mandara, pārijat, sarala, tamal, tala, kovidara, asana, arjuna, amra-jati (mango), kadamba, dhuli-kadamba, naga, punnaga, champaka, patala, ashoka, bakula, kunda and kurabaka. The entire hill is covered with such trees, which produce flowers with fragrant aromas.

There are other trees also are planted on the hill, such as the golden lotus flower, the cinnamon tree, malati, kubja, mallika and madhavi.

Kailash Hill also has trees such as kata, jackfruit, julara, banyan trees, plakṣas, nyagrodhas and trees producing asafetida. Also, there are trees of betel nuts and bhurja-patra, as well as rajapuga, blackberries and similar other trees.

There are mango trees, priyala, madhuka and inguda. Besides these, there are other trees, like thin bamboo, kichaka and varieties of other bamboo trees, all decorating the tract of Kailash Hill.

There are different kinds of lotus flowers, such as kumuda, utpala and shatapatra. The forest appears to be a decorated garden, and the small lakes are full of various kinds of birds who whisper very sweetly. There are many kinds of other animals also, like deer, monkeys, boars, lions, forest cows, forest asses, tigers, small deer, buffalo and many other animals, who are fully enjoying their lives.

There are varieties of deer, such as karnantra, ekapada, ashvasya, vrika and kasturi, the deer which bears musk. Besides the deer, there are many banana trees that are planted on the banks of the small hillside lakes very nicely.

There is a small lake named Alakananda in which Sati used to take her bath, and that lake is especially auspicious. All the demigods, after seeing the specific beauty of Kailash Hill, were struck with wonder at the great opulence to be found there.

Thus, the demigods saw the wonderfully beautiful region known as Alaka in the forest known as Saugandhika, which means 'full of fragrance'. The forest is known as Saugandhika because of its abundance of lotus flowers.

They also saw the two rivers named Nanda and Alakananda. These two rivers are sanctified by the dust of the lotus feet of the Supreme Lord, Govinda.

My dear Kshatta, Vidura, the celestial damsels, come down to those rivers in their aeroplanes with their husbands, and after enjoyment, they enter the water and enjoy sprinkling their husbands with water.

After the damsels of the heavenly planets bathe in the water, it becomes yellowish and fragrant due to the kumkum from their bodies. Thus the elephants come to bathe there with their wives, the she-elephants, and they also drink the water, although they are not thirsty.

The aeroplanes of the heavenly denizens are bedecked with pearls, gold and many valuable jewels. The heavenly denizens are compared to clouds in the sky decorated with occasional flashes of electric lightning.

While travelling, the demigods passed over the forest known as Saugandhika, which is full of varieties of flowers, fruits and desired trees. While passing over the forest, they also saw the regions of Yaksheshvara.

In that celestial forest, there were many birds whose necks were coloured reddish and whose sweet sounds mixed with the humming of the bees. The lakes were abundantly decorated with crying swans as well as strong-stemmed lotus flowers.

All these atmospheric influences unsettled the forest elephants who flocked together in the sandalwood forest, and the blowing wind agitated the minds of the damsels there for further enjoyment.

They also saw that the bathing *ghats*[29] and their staircases were made of vaidurya-mani. The water was full of lotus flowers. Passing by such lakes, the demigods reached a place where there was a great banyan tree.

That banyan tree was 800 miles high, and its branches spread over 600 miles around. The tree cast a fine shade, which permanently cooled the temperature, yet there was no noise of birds.

The demigods saw Lord Shiva sitting under that tree, which was competent to give perfection to mystic yogis and deliver all people. As grave as time eternal, he appeared to have given up all anger.

Lord Shiva sat there, surrounded by saintly persons like Kuvera, the master of the Guhyakas, and the four Kumaras, who were already liberated souls. Lord Shiva was grave and saintly.

The demigods saw Lord Shiva situated in his perfection as the master of the senses, knowledge, fruitive activities[30] and the path of achieving perfection. He was the friend of the entire world, and by virtue of his full affection for everyone, he was very auspicious.

He was seated on a deerskin and was practising all forms of austerity. Because his body was smeared with ashes, he looked like an evening cloud. On his hair was the sign of a half-moon, a symbolic representation.

He was speaking to all present, including the great Sage Narada, to whom he specifically spoke about the Absolute Truth.

---

[29] Riverfronts.

[30] Acts performed to fulfil material desires.

His left leg was placed on his right thigh, and his left hand was placed on his left thigh. (This sitting posture is called *virasana*.) In his right hand, he held rudraksh beads, and his finger was in the mode of argument.

All the sages and demigods, headed by Indra, offered their respectful obeisances unto Lord Shiva with folded hands. Lord Shiva was dressed in saffron garments and absorbed in trance, thus appearing to be the foremost of all sages.

Lord Shiva's lotus feet were worshipped by both the demigods and demons, but still, in spite of his exalted position, as soon as he saw that Lord Brahma was there among all the other demigods, he immediately stood up and offered him respect by bowing down and touching his lotus feet, just as Vamanadeva offered His respectful obeisances to Kashyap Muni.

All the sages who were sitting with Lord Shiva, such as Narada and others, also offered their respectful obeisances to Lord Brahma. After being so worshipped, Lord Brahma, smiling, began to speak to Lord Shiva.

This account gives a glimpse of the tranquil abode of Lord Shiva and that of Lord Shiva himself. The abode is serene, devotional and free from any miseries. Till we become pure enough to realize its true nature, we can simply relish the beauty through these descriptions and through the eyes of the great souls who have seen the truth.

Chapter 10

Shivaratri: The Night of Lord Shiva

Perhaps the most important festival associated with Lord Shiva is Shivaratri. Taken from two words—Shiv and *Ratri*—it translates to 'The Night of Lord Shiva'. There is a Shivaratri every month but the one that falls in the month of *Falgun* (February/March) is most special and is known as the Mahashivaratri. The most important of twelve monthly sacred festivals held throughout the year, Mahashivaratri is a time for fasting, prayers and offerings. Unlike most Vedic festivals, this unique event is celebrated at night.

The Legend

There are various interesting legends related to the festival of Mahashivaratri.

According to one legend, this day commemorates Lord Shiva's marriage to Mother Parvati, who performed severe penances for a long time to please Lord Shiva to get him as a husband. Finally, she succeeded, and on this day, their marriage took place. Hence, on this day, unmarried women pray for a husband like Lord Shiva, who is considered to be the ideal husband.

Another legend says that during the creation of the universe, Lord Shiva incarnated in the Universe through Lord Brahma on this night.

It is also believed that on this night, Lord Shiva performed his cosmic dance of creation, the *Tandav* dance, when he heard the news of his wife, Goddess Sati's, immolation at her father's house.

Another popular Shivaratri legend mentioned in Linga Purana states that it was on Shivaratri that Lord Shiva manifested himself in the form of a linga. Hence, the day is considered to be extremely auspicious by Lord Shiva devotees, who celebrate it as the grand night of Lord Shiva.

Another belief related to the origin of this sacred day is associated with the celestial event known as the churning of the milk ocean (*samudra manthan*) involving both gods and demons. This fight produced the immortal nectar in the end. But along with it, it had also produced, in the beginning, the most poisonous venom ever, known as the Halahala. The poison could destroy the universe and Lord Shiva, for the welfare of everyone, drank it. The poison was so potent that Lord Shiva continued to suffer from immense pain. As part of the therapy, the heavenly physicians advised the gods to keep Lord Shiva awake during the night. Thus, Gods kept a vigil in contemplation of Lord Shiva. To amuse Lord Shiva and keep him awake, the gods took turns performing various dances and playing music. As the day broke out, Lord Shiva, pleased with their devotion, blessed them all. Shivaratri is the celebration of this event, by which Lord Shiva saved the world. Since then, on this day and night, devotees fast, keep vigil, sing glories of the Lord and meditate the entire night.

But whatever the actual reason may be, the fact remains that it is an important day to be celebrated by remembering and worshipping Lord Shiva.

Rituals Associated with Mahashivaratri

The festival combines all-day fasting and an all-night vigil. During daylight hours, devotees rise early and take a ritualistic bath. After these ablutions, they head over to the nearest temple dedicated to Lord Shiva to make offerings of milk, yoghurt, honey, ghee, sugar and water.

In homes and temples throughout India, the sacred mantra of Lord Shiva is chanted, special worship is held, incense is burned, lamps are lit, and streams of pilgrims continue to appear during the day and into the night. Through it all, devotees maintain a solemn fast until the following morning.

During the festival, unmarried women observe this fast in the hope that they will find a partner, while married women observe the fast to give thanks and maintain the balance of harmony in their marriage.

Chapter 11

Rudraksha: The Sacred Bead

One of the most prominent things that remind us of Lord Shiva instantly is the *rudraksha*. The word 'rudraksha' is made up of two words: *rudra and aksha*. Rudra means Lord Shiva and aksha refers to eyes or teardrops from an eye.

The History of Origin

Rudraksha originated from the tears of Lord Shiva. According to Devi Bhagavata Purana, chapter 11, VII khanda, Maya, a demon, performed severe penance along with Taraka and Vidhyunmali to achieve immortality. Finally, they got a boon with the condition that they could be killed only by a single arrow from Lord Shiva's bow, when that arrow burns the three cities in which they live.

Maya, designated as the architect of the demonic race, built three airborne cities. These cities floated such that they converged into a single line only on the day of Pushya Nakshatra, a conjunction occurring once in a million years. Taraka's fort was made of iron, Vidhyunmali's was made of copper and Maya's was made of gold.

Very soon, the *Asuras*[31] took over the entire universe. As the devas were subdued, they prayed to Lord Shiva to fight for them and set them free from the reign of the Asuras. Lord Shiva acceded to their prayer and asked them to wait for an opportune moment.

At the end of the stipulated time period, Lord Shiva fashioned his weapons and accessories for war from various cosmic elements. The moment the three aerial cities converged, Lord Shiva mounted his chariot and with Lord Brahma as the charioteer, he sped upwards. He took out his bow and hit the converged cities with a single arrow. The cosmic arrow then destroyed the three cities simultaneously.

One version of the incident maintains that, finally, when everything was ready for the invasion, the devas felt proud thinking that only with their help was Lord Shiva capable of destroying the *Tripuras*.[32] But to the astonishment of all, Lord Shiva didn't use any of the war machinery arranged by the devas. Lord Shiva laughed and due to that laughter, the three *puras*[33] were destroyed. The arrogance of the devas who claimed that without their help, Lord Shiva would not be able to destroy the Tripuras, was vanquished.

After the demolition of the Tripuras, Lord Shiva returned to the Himalayas. There, when he closed his eyes

---

[31] Demons.

[32] The three cities.

[33] Cities.

and meditated for some time and then opened his eyes, a few droplets of tears fell from them onto the earth. The place on earth where the tears fell subsequently gave rise to Rudraksha trees.

According to another version, after several years of meditation, when Lord Shiva opened his eyes, he witnessed the suffering of humanity. Tears of compassion welled up in his eyes. When these tears fell to the ground, Rudraksha trees sprouted from them.

As per yet another version, when Goddess Sati immolated herself after her father Daksha humiliated Lord Shiva, he shed tears of unimaginable grief. The grief-stricken Lord Shiva circumambulated the world along with Sati's body. Seeing him roaming like a madman, immersed in sorrow, Lord Vishnu chopped Sati Devi's body into fifty-two parts to cultivate a mood of detachment in Lord Shiva. As long as the body was around, Lord Shiva could not give it up. Wherever these parts fell, they turned into Shakti peethas and wherever Lord Shiva's tears fell, Rudraksha trees emerged.

Chapter 12

Bel Patra: The Sacred Leaf

Just as tulsi is very dear to Lord Krishna, bel patra, also known as bilva leaf, is very dear to Lord Shiva. It is one of the six ritualistic essentials offered to Lord Shiva on the day of Mahashivaratri. After the Rudraksha beads, it is bel patra that is dearest to Mahadeva. In Shiva Puja, these leaves are offered unto the shivaling along with the chanting of *Mahamrityunjaya*[34] and other Shiva mantras.

The History of Origin

The Skanda Purana's 'Tirth Mahatmya' or Chapter 250, mentions that droplets of Goddess Parvati's sweat once fell on the Mandrachal mountain and led to the growth of the bel or bilva plant.

The Skanda Purana narrates the following incident:

Once, the splendid daughter of the mountains, Parvati, the goddess, felt felt tired while playing sports on

---

[34] That which conquers death.

the Mandar mountain. Drops of sweat appeared on her forehead. As she wiped them off, a drop fell on the ground. That drop became a great tree on that exalted mountain.

Sometime later, once again, she came to that place in the course of her sports. On seeing this wonderful tree in the forest, she was surprised. It was evident from her eyes that beamed with excitement.

She then asked her female companions, Jaya and Vijaya: 'What is this great divine tree shining in the centre of the forest? It appears very beautiful. Indeed, it gives great delight.'

Jaya said: 'O goddess, this tree has originated from your own body, from a drop of your sweat. Do name this tree soon. If it is worshipped, it will destroy sins.'

Parvati said: 'Since this great tree pierced through the ground and rose near me, let it be named Bilva.

If anyone approaches this tree devoutly and collects the leaves, he shall certainly become a king of the earth.

If anyone with perfect faith worships me with its leaves, he will realize whatever desire he may cherish.

If a person, after seeing the leaves of bel, offers respect, I shall undoubtedly be the bestower of wealth on him.

If anyone makes up his mind to eat the tip of the leaves, thousands of his sins will perish automatically.

If a man places the tip of the leaf on his head, no torture of Yama will give him pain.'

After saying this, the delighted Goddess Parvati went to her abode accompanied by her companions and ganas.

The Purana mentions that Goddess Parvati resides in the bel tree in all Her forms. She resides as Girija at its root, Dakshayani on its stem, Maheshwari on its branches, Goddess Parvati on its leaves and Katyayani on its fruit.

Gauri has been mentioned as present on its bark, Aparna in the middle of the bark, Durga in the flower, and Uma in the branches and twigs.

At the behest of Girija, 9 crore shaktis have stationed themselves on all its thorns for the sake of protecting living beings.

As Mother Parvati is very dear to Lord Shiva and as she resides in bel leaves, Lord Shiva, who sees her presence in them, becomes very pleased with the offering of bel leaves.

When one offers bel leaves to Lord Shiva during Shivaratri, the merit obtained is equivalent to 1000 yajnas. 100 lotus flowers are equal to one neel kamal[35] and 1000 neel kamals are equal to one bel patra. Thus, bel patra is the easiest way to please Lord Shiva. Even the most terrible karmic reactions are destroyed when you offer bel leaves to the Shivling on Mahashivaratri.

Another legend has it that when Lord Shiva drank the Halahala poison that came out during the churning of the ocean, for the welfare of the world, his throat turned blue. This was where he got the name, Neelkanth. It became an ornament on his transcendental body.

The effect of this poison was so terrible that Lord Shiva's head started heating up and his throat started burning. The celestial Gods poured water on his head, which did provide

---

[35] Blue lotus.

some relief, but the burning of his throat did not subside. It was then that the Gods fed him bel leaves, which provided instant relief. Thus, bel leaves hold a special importance in the worship of Lord Shiva.

Chapter 13

Varanasi: The Capital of Lord Shiva

We cannot talk about Lord Shiva without talking about Varanasi.

Also known as Kashi, it is one of the most ancient cities of learning. This was a place where hundreds of enlightened beings lived at a time. In every street, we had an enlightened being to meet.

Having stood the test of time for over 5000 years, a city that has seen the world turn, tides change, and generations of humans take birth and perish, Varanasi or Banaras, is said to be one of the oldest inhabited cities in the world.

There are supposed to be 2000 temples in Varanasi. It is 125 km east of Prayag, on the bank of the Ganga.

In Mark Twain's words, 'Benaras is older than history, older than tradition, older even than legend, and looks twice as old as all of them put together.'[36]

---

[36] Sanya Dhingra, 'After puja in Gyanvapi, Banaras, the city "older than history", is quietly changing', ThePrint, 12 February 2024, https://theprint.in/ground-reports/after-puja-in-gyanvapi-banaras-the-city-older-than-history-is-quietly-changing/1962652/.

What draws millions of pilgrims from all over the world to the city of Varanasi is that it is one of the holiest of the seven sacred cities in India. It is called the spiritual capital of India because this magnificent city of learning radiates endless energy. Despite witnessing ancient civilizations come and go over centuries, Varanasi is still alive, unabashedly colourful, vibrant, and wonderfully rich in history and legends.

Varanasi, also popularly known as Banaras or Kashi, has been given several poetic adjectives such as 'the city of temples', 'the holy city of India', 'the religious capital of India', 'the city of light', 'the city of learning', 'the culture capital of India' and more.

Varanasi, the holy city of light, shines bright, both physically and metaphorically. It is believed that a single dip in the holy waters of the Ganga can wash away a lifetime of sins.

According to Puranic history, Varanasi was founded by Lord Shiva and became his favourite abode. In one verse of the ancient religious text of Skanda Purana, Lord Shiva says, 'The three worlds form one city of mine, and Kāśī is my royal palace therein.' The Kashi Khanda of Skanda Purana provides a detailed description of the glories of this holy place.

In Varanasi, the most natural and inevitable cycle of life and death is celebrated and revered with much gusto. Also known as *Mahashamshana* or 'the great cremation grounds', this holy city humbles you by bringing you face to face with the balance of life and death.

Many old people, desiring liberation, come to Varanasi to leave their bodies in this holy city and be cremated at the burning ghats along the river Ganga. It is believed that anyone who dies in Varanasi attains *moksha*.[37]

A boat ride across the sacred Ganga perfectly captures the spirit of Varanasi. Countless candlelit paper boats with flowers carrying people's prayers float their way across the waters. While countless pilgrims take a holy dip in the waters, others meditate in solitude and the rest bow their heads in prayer along the ghats.

As the sun goes down, the evening ritual of worship, called the Ganga *Aarti*,[38] unfolds.

Varanasi has been the original hub of art, culture, spirituality and music. Many prominent Indian saints and philosphers such as Rupa Goswami, Sanatan Goswami, Shri Jiva Goswami, Shri Shankaracharya, Shri Tulsidas and Kabir, poets and writers like Munshi Premchand, and musicians such as Ravi Shankar and Girija Devi and the Supreme Lord Chaitanya Mahaprabhu have lived in Varanasi. Several major figures of the Bhakti movement were born in Varanasi, including Kabir and Ravidas.

Varanasi is home to the Kashi Vishwanath temple, one of the most important places of worship in the country, considered to be one of the twelve *jyotirlingas*[39] of Lord Shiva, holding great significance in the spiritual history of India.

---

[37] Freedom/liberation from the cycle of birth and death.

[38] A Hindu ceremony in which lights with wicks soaked in ghee are lit and offered up to one or more deities.

[39] Shrines where Lord Shiva is worshipped as a fiery column of light.

The Name

The name 'Varanasi' was derived from the tract of land lying between the confluence of rivers Varuna and Asi. Hence, Varun-asi or Varanasi. Varuna and Asi join the Ganga River on the north and south borders of the city. The Varuna River is a minor tributary of the Ganga, which is named after the god Varuna, the god of water. The Varuna River starts from Melhum at Phulpur in Allahabad district, flows east-to-southeast for 106 kilometres via Bhadohi, Mirzapur and Jaunpur, and enters Varanasi in order to finally merge with the Ganga at Sarai Mohana.

The rivulet that borders the city of Varanasi at its south and joins the Ganga at Asi Ghat is known as Assi or Asi River.

There are numerous references to the Asi Ghat in the ancient works of literature. It was at the Asi Ghat where the famous Indian poet saint, Tulsidas, had written the much-celebrated Ramacharitmanas.

Varanasi is said to be located between two confluences: one of Ganga and Varuna, and the other of Ganga and Asi, which always remained a rivulet rather than a river. The distance between these two confluences is around 4 km. The pilgrims regard a round trip between these two places as a religious ritual, which ends with a visit to the Sakshi Vinayak Temple and is called *panchkoshi yatra* (a fifty-mile journey).

According to the Padma Purana, the Varuna and the Asi are two holy rivers, and between them is a holy land. According to Lord Shiva Purana, there is no other place more exceptional on earth.

Varanasi is situated between the Varuna, which flows into the Ganga on the north and the Asi, which joins the Ganga on the south. In the Rig Veda, the city was referred to as Kasi or Kashi, which means 'the luminous one'.

There are references to Asi Ghat in Matsya Purana, Agni Purana, Kurma Purana and Padma Purana. According to the Puranas, Goddess Durga had thrown her sword after slaying the demons Shumbha and Nishumbha. At the place where the sword fell, a big stream gushed, known as the Asi River.

Long ago, Varuna was recognized as the lifeline of Varanasi. The pure and medicinal properties of the water nourished various types of herbs on its banks, and the river maintained the water level of the city. The farmers of this area were dependent on its water for drinking, irrigation and cattle. In the present scenario, the situation has changed drastically—the Varuna is one of the most polluted rivers in India.

Steeped in tradition and mythological legacy, Kashi is the 'original ground' created by Lord Shiva and Goddess Parvati, upon which they stood at the beginning of time. The city is the microcosm of India, a city of traditional, classical culture, glorified and sanctified by religion. It has always attracted a large number of pilgrims and worshippers. To be in Varanasi is an experience in itself—an experience in self-discovery, and the eternal harmony of the body and soul.

It is said that the first Shiva jyotirlinga, the fiery pillar of light, came through the earth here and flared into the sky. Therefore, Varanasi is also called Kashi or 'city of light'. Kashi is mentioned in the Mahabharata, Ramayana, Srimad Bhagavatam and the Puranas, which date back 5000 years, as the foremost city of Lord Shiva. The Muslims later gave it the name Benaras. After Independence, the old name, Varanasi, was given to the city again.

Religious texts use many epithets to refer to Varanasi, such as Kāśikā (Sanskrit: the shining one), Avimukta (Sanskrit: never forsaken' by Lord Shiva), Ānandavana (Sanskrit: the forest of bliss) and Rudravāsa (Sanskrit: the place where Rudra/Śiva resides).

The Ganga, which normally flows southeast, reverses its course and flows north for a while in Varanasi, which is considered very auspicious. There is a fifty-mile parikrama path that goes around this sacred city. There are eighty-one bathing ghats and other holy *kunds*, or sacred tanks.

The Kashi Vishwanath Temple

Also known as the Golden Temple, the Kashi Vishwanath temple is dedicated to Lord Shiva, the presiding deity of the city.

In Varanasi, people focus their devotion on the shivaling in the temple more than on the ghats of the Ganga. The Kashi Vishwanath temple is considered to be the holiest of Lord Shiva temples. It stands on the western bank of the holy river Ganga and is one of the twelve jyotirlingas. The main deity is known by the name Vishwanatha or Vishweshwara, which means ruler of the universe. The temple town, which claims to be the oldest living city in the world, and has 3500 years of documented history, is also called Kashi. Hence, the temple is popularly known as the Kashi Vishwanath temple. The temple's structure had been destroyed and reconstructed several

times in history. The last structure was demolished
by Aurangzeb in 1669, who constructed the Gyanvapi
Mosque on its site. The current structure was built on
an adjacent site by the Maratha monarch, Ahilya Bai
Holkar of Indore in 1780. Since 1983, the temple has been
managed by the government of Uttar Pradesh. During the
religious occasion of Shivaratri, the Kashi Naresh (king of
Kashi) is the chief officiating priest and no other person
or priest is allowed to enter the sanctum sanctorum. It is
only after he performs his religious functions that others
are allowed to enter.

A simple glimpse of the jyotirlinga is a spiritually
purifying moment that leads one's life towards the path
of transformation, knowledge and bhakti. Vishweshwara
Jyotirlinga has a very special and unique significance in the
spiritual history of India. According to the traditions, the
merits earned by the darshan of other jyotirlinga in various
parts of India are consolidated for devotees in a single visit
to the Kashi Vishwanath temple.

The temple has been visited by many great personalities
such as Lord Chaitanya, Lord Nityananda, Adi
Shankaracharya, Goswami Tulsidas, Guru Nanak and Srila
Bhakti Siddhant Saraswati Thakur. It attracts visitors not
only from India but abroad as well, which symbolizes man's
desire to live in peace and harmony with one another.

In 1839, two domes of the temple were covered with
gold donated by the Punjab Kesari Maharaja Ranjeet Singh.

The temple opens daily at 2.30 a.m. The *mangala*
aarti[40] takes place from 3 to 4 a.m. All ticket holders are
permitted to join.

---

[40] The first and early morning aarti.

From 4 to 11 a.m.: General darshan is allowed.

11.30 to noon: Mid-day bhoga aarti is done.

Again, 12 noon to 7 p.m.: Devotees are free to have darshan.

From 7 to 8.30 p.m.: Evening saptarishi aarti is done after which darshan is again possible until 9 p.m. when *shringar*/bhoga aarti commences.

After 9 p.m.: Darshan from outside the doors is possible.

Shayana[41] aarti starts at 10.30 p.m. The temple closes at 11 p.m.

Ganga's Arrival in Kashi

Once, when the king of Koshala, Sagara, was performing the *Ashwamedha Yajna*,[42] he lost track of his sacrificial horse. To find the horse, he sent his 60,000 sons. The sons searched for the horse in every corner of the earth and destroyed everything that came in their path. At last, they reached Sage Kapila's ashram and found the horse tied to a tree. They accused the sage of stealing the horse. As a result of this offence to sage Kapila, all 60,000 sons were burned to ashes. King Sagara, who was anxiously waiting for his sons, eventually sent his grandson, Anshuman, to search for them. When he reached Kapila's ashram, the sage told him that only through the presence of the sacred river Ganga can all sons be purified and delivered.

Many kings of the dynasty performed austere penances to bring Ganga to earth, but they could not succeed.

---

[41] The Lord is put to sleep.

[42] A powerful wish-fulfilling Vedic ceremony.

As time passed, their curse multiplied and it started to destroy the once-great Koshala kingdom. It was King Bhagirath, who spurred into action and performed penance for 1000 years to please Lord Brahma, thus bringing Ganga to earth. Lord Brahma was aware that the force of the river was so destructive that the earth would not be able to hold it. Therefore, he told Bhagirath to pray to Lord Shiva. After a year of penance, Lord Shiva appeared and told Bhagirath that his wish would be fulfilled. When Ganga was falling from heaven, everybody was so afraid that everything would be destroyed. Ganga did come with full force. But as she was about to hit the earth, Lord Shiva captured her in his *jata*.[43] Ganga was helpless and unable to come out of it. When Bhagirath saw this, he prayed to Lord Shiva again, and Lord Shiva finally released Ganga.

Ganga now flowed behind King Bhagirath, giving liberation to all his ancestors by flowing over their ashes. Before this, King Bhagirath also got her on the way to Varanasi. Since Varanasi is the eternal abode of Lord Shiva, to pay homage to the city, Ganga decided to change course and started flowing northward. In Indian culture, a place where two rivers join is sacred. In Varanasi, there are three such points, thus making it even more auspicious.

The Ghats

The spectacular 4-km sweep of the ghats is a unique sight, best viewed at dawn, in that soft, first light when the river and ghats appear timeless. From dawn to dusk, life unfolds

---

[43] Matted hair.

in panoramic detail here, and a steady stream of devotees arrive in thousands on auspicious days to perform rituals at the Ganga. The extensive stretches of ghats in Varanasi enhance the riverfront with a multitude of shrines, temples and palaces.

The ghats are best approached by the Dashasawamedha ghat, where boats are available for hire.

The Ganga ghats are the most popular pilgrimage spot of Varanasi and act as centres of music and learning. There is a great tradition of pilgrimage in the holy city of Kashi and the most sacred path is that of the panchkoshi parikrama, the fifty-mile path with a radius of fifty miles that covers 108 shrines along the way, with the Panchkoshi temple as its main shrine.

Many of the ghats were constructed under the patronage of the Marathas, Shindes (Scindias), Holkars, Bhonsles and Peshwas. A morning boat ride on the Ganga across the ghats is a popular tourist attraction.

Every year, countless pilgrims come to Varanasi. The three most important ghats are Manikarnika, Dasaswamedha and Panchaganga. To bathe at these three ghats is called *Tri-tirtha* yatra. Also important are Asi Sangam and Varuna Sangam. To bathe in these five places is called the *panchatirtha* yatra. You are supposed to bathe in these five ghats in a certain order. First, you bathe in Asi Ghat, then Dasaswamedha Ghat, then the ghat by the Adi Keshava Temple near the Varuna River, then Panchaganga, and then Manikarnika. After taking a bath at these five places, most pilgrims go for the darshan of Visvanath, Annapurna and Sakshi Vinayaka (witnessing Lord Ganesh). It is said that if you bathe in these five places, all on the same day and in this order, you will not get another material body but liberation. You can do the panchatirtha yatra by boat, but it is better to do it on foot.

Varanasi has at least eighty-four ghats, most of which are used for bathing by pilgrims and spiritually significant puja ceremonies, while a few are used exclusively as Hindu cremation sites.

The Main Ghats

1. Asi Ghat

Asi Ghat is an important ghat of Varanasi. It traditionally constitutes the southern end of the conventional city. The confluence place of river Ganga and Asi is known as Asi or Assi ghat. In Kashi khanda, it is said that one gets pious credits of all the *tirthas*[44] by taking a dip here. It is also said that it was here that Saint Tulsidas sat and wrote the Ramcharitmanas. After the nineteenth century, Asi Ghat was divided into five Ghats i.e. Asi, Gangamahal, Rewan, tulsi and Bhadaini.

2. Dasashwamedha Ghat

This is the most ancient and bustling ghat. Lord Brahma performed the ten-horse sacrifice (*dasa-asvamedha*) for King Divodasa at this site. The southern part of the ghat was reconstructed in 1740 by Peshwa Bajirao I, and later in 1774 by Ahilyabai Holkar of Indore. This is the main bathing ghat, so it is generally

---

[44] Religious places.

extremely crowded. It is said that bathing here gives one the same merits as received by doing the ten-horse sacrifice that was performed here. The area around this ghat is the main centre of activity in the city, especially for pilgrims and tourists.

This ghat is full of pilgrims bathing in the holy Ganga. On certain auspicious days, up to 30,000 pilgrims may take a bath here.

Ganga puja is also performed every evening on Dasasvamedha Ghat.

3. Manikarnika Ghat

This is popularly called 'the great cremation ground' (Mahashamshana).

It is said that Lord Shiva chants the *Taraka* mantra of Lord Rama ('Prayer for the crossing cycle of birth and death') in the ear of whoever dies in Varanasi. The Manikarnika (jewelled earring) ghat is said to be given this name because, while dancing, Lord Shiva's earring fell into a well right next to the ghat. In the vicinity are shrines of Manikarnikesvara, Mahesvara (open-air lingam at the ghat), the Siddha and Manikarna Vinayakas. The temple of Manikarnikesvara can be reached from the ghat by taking a steep ascending lane to the south of the *kunda*.[45]

Manikarnika ghat is considered to be the holiest of all the ghats. Normally, the cremation ground is situated on the outskirts as it is polluted. Here, the burning ghat is in the middle of the city, because death in Varanasi is considered a great blessing. It is said to bring bad luck if one mourns

---

[45] A small tank or a lake.

or cries for the dead. At any given time, there may be half a dozen bodies burning here. The bodies are first placed in the Ganga before being cremated.

The Manikarnika Kund is said to be so old that it was present before King Bhagirath brought the Ganga to Varanasi. This kund is also called the Chakra-Pushkarini Kund or 'Discus–Lotus Pond'. At one time, this kund was a huge lake. It is thought to come from a source separate from the Ganga, an underground river that comes directly from Gaumukh, which is the source of the Ganga. It is believed that this well was dug by Lord Vishnu with his disc (chakra) and filled with water as his first act of creation. There is an image of Lord Vishnu in the northern wall of the kund. Offerings of milk, sandalwood, sweets and bel flowers, which are sacred to Lord Shiva, are offered in the well. In October or November, there is a good chance the kund will be covered by dirt, because when the Ganga floods during the rainy season (June–September), dirt from the Ganga covers up the kund. It is then dug out each year in November.

Lord Vishnu's footprints (*charana paduka*) are located at Chakra-Pushkarini, between the Manikarnika Kund and the river. For 7000 years, Lord Vishnu is believed to have stayed and performed penance on this spot.

4. Panchaganga Ghat

Beneath this ghat, the Ganga, Yamuna, Saraswati, Kirana and Dhutapapa Rivers are said to meet. Only the first one is visible, and the others have either disappeared or are assumed to exist in an unmanifested form. The Panchaganga Ghat is one of the five main ghats in Varanasi.

It is considered especially auspicious to bathe here during the sacred month of *Kartik* (October–November) and most importantly, on the full moon day of Kartika. The merit and glory of this ghat is described in the Kasi khanda (59;116–44). This was the chief resort of a great teacher of Vedanta, Ramananda (1299–1411), whom Kabir, a great reformist and bhakti poet, accepted as his guru.

Tulsidas Goswami (1547–1623) was initially living (circa 1580s–1590s) at this ghat, where he composed the famous *Bindu-patrika* ('The petition to Rama'), describing the glory of Bindu Madhava temple.

At this ghat is the large Alamgir mosque built by Aurangzeb in the seventeenth century, after he destroyed the major Bindu Madhava temple that existed here. The present deity of Bindu Madhava is in a small temple near the mosque. It is located just above the Panchaganga Ghat. If you are taking a boat by yourself, you can have the boat stop here and walk up to the temple.

The Legend of Bindu Madhav

There is a beautiful story of how Lord Vishnu came to be known as Bindu Madhava.

As per the directions of Lord Shiva, Lord Vishnu travelled from Mandarachal to Kashi with a divine mission of making King Divodas leave Kashi.

After having accomplished his mission, Lord Vishnu was enjoying the serene beauty of Kashi, Panchanada Tirth, Padodak Tirth and other places. At Panchanada Tirth, he came across one extremely lean-looking sage who was undergoing austerity.

Lord Vishnu, in his divine form, approached the sage whose name was Agni Bindu and stood in front of him. On seeing the Lord personally appearing, the sage was ecstatic and prostrated before the Lord while singing his praises.

The sage addressed the Lord by various names like Mukunda, Madusudan, Madhav, Narayan, Rama Bhadran, Chatur Bhuj, Janardhan, etc. The sage also mentioned that those who worship Lord Vishnu with tulsi leaves or garlands made of tulsi leaves would get lots of blessings.

After having sung all the praises about Lord Vishnu, Agni Bindu Rishi stood silently with folded hands. Lord Vishnu asked the sage to seek any divine boon. The sage sought only one thing: that Lord Vishnu should always be available for his worship in the vicinity of this Panchanada Tirth.

Lord Vishnu granted his wish. He further stated that Kashi is a very sacred and pious city and devotees can achieve several kinds of mystic perfections by staying in Kashi, and that he would stay in Kashi as long as Kashi was present. Kashi, of course, would never be destroyed as it was a holy city situated atop the trishul[46] of Lord Shiva. Therefore, even a *mahapralay*[47] would not be able to destroy the city.

Agni Bindu Rishi was extremely happy with this and sought one more divine boon from Lord Vishnu. He desired that Lord Vishnu should not just appear here, but also appear with a name connected to him.

---

[46] Trident.

[47] Great deluge.

Lord Vishnu agreed to the request of the sage. He stated that henceforth He (the Lord) would be known as Bindu Madhav in Panchanada Tirtha. His presence would make the place extremely sacred, and the devotees who bathed here would be blessed with wealth and prosperity.

This place, which is capable of cleansing all sins, is now called Bindu Tirtha. A person may have committed various sins, knowingly or unknowingly, but if during the Kartik month, he religiously bathes in Panchanada and worships Bindu Madhav, he will attain liberation.

Lord Shiva himself regularly takes a bath in this holy place during the Kartik month.

Lord Vishnu further stated that He (the Lord) was called Aadi Madhav in *Satya Yug*, Ananda Madhav in *Treta Yug*, and Shree Madhav in *Dwapar Yug*. In Kaliyuga, the Lord will be known by the name of Bindu Madhav.

The festival deity or the *utsava* deity[48] of Lord Bindu Madhav was found in the holy Ganga at Varanasi by Shri Madhavendra Tirtha Swami while he was having a bath at the ghats. During this period, the main deity of Lord Bindu Madhav was transferred to the Moola *mutt*[49]of Kashi Mutt for protection from the invaders. However, the festival *murti*[50] went missing for a long time. Shri Madhavendra Tirtha Swami found it and reinstalled it in the temple. It is this festival deity of Lord Bindu Madhav who partakes in all the festivals. He not only restarted the different festivals

---

[48] The deity that is taken out for all festival rituals such as bathing, procession, etc.

[49] Moola means original/central and mutt means monastery.

[50] Deity.

but is credited with starting the *Brahma Rathothsava*[51] on Ram Navami.

Lord Chaitanya Mahaprabhu, the *Yugavatar* (the avatar for this yuga and a combined form of Radha–Lord Krishna) who appeared in 1486, also bathed at the Panchaganga Ghat and visited the old temple of Bindu Madhava. While staying in Varanasi on his way back from Vrindavan, Lord Chaitanya became the guest of the great Vaishnava devotees, Tapan Mishra and Chandrasekhar. It was here that he met another great Vaishnava Acharya Sanatana Goswami and also converted Prakashananda Saraswati, the great impersonalist (who considered God's form to be an illusion and believed God is not a person) and his followers, to Vaishnavism while staying at Varanasi.

5. Adi Keshava Ghat

This ghat is also referred to as the Vedesvara Ghat.

This is assumed to be the oldest and the original (*Adi*) site of Lord Vishnu (Keshava).

The Adi Keshava Vishnu temple is located where the Ganga meets the Varuna River, in the northern part of the city.

The five holy spots represent the bodily parts of the Lord: Asi is the head, Dasasvamedha is the chest, Manikarnika is the navel, Panchaganga is the thighs and Adi Kesava is the feet.

Lord Vishnu first placed his holy feet here in Varanasi—his footprints in the Adi Kesava temple symbolize

---

[51] A chariot festival for the deity.

that occasion. There is another set of footprints at the Manikarnika ghat.

The appearance day (Jayanti) of Vamana (the Dwarf or the fifth incarnation of Lord Vishnu among the ten) is celebrated on a massive scale in the Adi Kesava temple on the twelfth day (*dvadashi tithi*) of Bhadrapada (August–September).

Chapter 14

The Legend of Amarnath

One of the most holy sites connected to Lord Shiva and visited by millions every year is the most glorious Amarnath in the Himalayas, situated at the height of 3,888 m (12,756 ft). 'Amar' means immortal and 'nath' means master or guardian. What makes it so special and where does it get its name from? It was here that Lord Shiva narrated the secret of immortality to Mother Parvati.

Legend has it that once, the great sage Narada visited Kailash, the home of Lord Shiva and Goddess Parvati. Narada was also the spiritual master of Goddess Parvati and thus, upon his arrival, she joyfully welcomed him and had him sit on a sacred seat. While conversing Narada, who is an expert in manifesting the will of the Supreme Lord Krishna/Lord Vishnu, thereby adding sweetness to the Lord's pastimes through his various intrigues, asked Mother Parvati whether everything was alright with her and whether Lord Shiva was taking good care of her. When Mother Parvati said yes, Narada again asked, 'Does Mahadeva share all his secrets with you?' She said yes, even though the question made her a little hesitant. Narada was like, 'Really?' She grew suspicious, and he continued, 'Then tell me why does he wear that garland of skulls around his neck? Whose skulls are these? Has he ever told you?' Mother Paravati could not reply. She said, 'No, he has never shared. But why not?' Seeing that he had managed to sow a seed of doubt in the Goddess's mind, Narada smiled and left, chanting 'Narayan, Narayan!'

We must remember that whatever Narada Muni does is as per the will of the Supreme Lord. He is the incarnation of the Lord's mind. Whenever he seems to be doing something, it is to be understood that some plan of the Lord is about to be manifested.

Meanwhile, Goddess Parvati was eagerly awaiting Lord Shiva's arrival to pour her heart out and question him for having kept this secret. When Lord Shiva arrived, she did not speak initially. When Lord Shiva saw her in a sulking mood, he enquired as to what was the cause and whether anyone had visited her in his absence. When she mentioned Narada's name, Lord Shiva smiled, knowing him to be the cause of some mischief. He called her to him, requested her to share what was in her heart and assured her that he would do anything to please her. Feeling secure now, Mother Parvati asked him the purpose behind wearing the munda mala.[52] To this, the Lord replied: 'These skulls are yours from your many past births. Every time you die, a head gets attached to this garland and hence, it continues to grow. The number of skulls indicates the number of times you have left your body and been reborn.'

---

52 Garland of skulls.

Confused upon hearing this, Mother Parvati enquired as to why is it that she dies and is destroyed every time while he (Lord Shiva) is immortal. Lord Shiva answered that the secret to his immortality was the 'Amar Katha'.

Curious now, the Goddess also wanted to know this secret. Refusing at first, Lord Shiva decided to reveal the secret to her upon her insistence. But the secret could not be told in a place like Kailash where many other associates resided. Not everyone was qualified to hear it. Thus, they left Mount Kailash and started looking for a secluded place where no living being could hear it.

Lord Shiva, to have complete seclusion, left others behind too at various places. For instance, Nandi, the bull was left at Pahalgam (initially known as Bailgam, the village of the bull) and ordered to guard the location and not allow any living creatures hereafter. It is therefore believed that one must walk on foot from Pahalgam as the Lord started his journey here. The Lord left the moon from his forehead at Chandanwari and the serpent Vasuki around his neck on the banks of Lake Sheshnag (or Anantnag). Lord Ganesha was left at Mahagunas Parvat, also called MahaLord Ganesh Mountain.

In addition, the five elements of nature—earth, water, air, fire and sky were left at Panchtarni.

Eventually, they came to the Amarnath cave.

Then, he created *Kalagni Rudra*[53] and ordered him to set a fire and eliminate every living thing in and around the cave. Then Lord Shiva took Goddess Parvati inside the cave to narrate to her the 'Amar Katha'. After entering

---

[53] A destructive form of Lord Shiva resembling fire.

the cave, the Lord started meditating in the lotus posture while sitting on deer skin. At an auspicious time, he started narrating the secret, which was nothing but the Bhagavat Katha—the divine pastimes of the Supreme Lord. But as a matter of chance, there was an egg that was lying beneath the deerskin that remained protected. It had been saved since it was believed to be non-living. Moreover, it was protected by the Lord's deer skin, upon which he was sitting. From this point onwards, there are two parallel legends about Amarnath.

One legend says that a parrot hatched from the egg and heard the narration. Mother Parvati happened to fall asleep, but the parrot enjoyed listening to the divine narration and kept making a humming sound. Lord Shiva, thinking Mother Parvati was awake, did not stop speaking. However, when the Lord completed the narration, he realized what had happened. Infuriated, he ran behind the parrot with his mighty trident to kill him. The parrot flew away quickly and reached Badrikashrama. Finding no other way to escape, the parrot entered the open mouth of Sage Vyasa's wife and went into her womb.

Meanwhile, Lord Shiva, with angry eyes, showed up with the trident in his hand and pointed it at the sage's wife. Sage Vyasa was bewildered and requested Lord Shiva to calm down and tell him what the matter was. Lord Shiva related what had happened and how this parrot was not qualified but still heard the 'Bhagavat Katha', which has the power to grant immortality. Hearing this, Sage Vyasa smiled and said, 'My dear Lord! The very fact that he heard the narration is proof that he was qualified because no one can hear the Supreme Lord's pastimes (katha) without having the necessary qualification.' Lord Shiva understood what the sage said and thus, satisfied, left the scene. This same parrot was later born as Shukadev Goswami, who narrated the same Shrimad Bhagavatam to King Parikshit for seven days.

The other legend says that from the egg, a pair of pigeons hatched, who listened to the secrets of Amar Katha and became immortal. Even to this day, one can see a pair of pigeons visit Amarnath. It is believed that after this incident, Lord Shiva ordained that anybody who listened to the Amar Katha or visited the Amarnath cave would attain moksha.

Thus, the cave got its name as Amarnath—the place where the secret of immortality was spoken.

Chapter 15

Different Roles

1. Bhootnath: The Lord of The Ghosts

Lord Shiva, or Rudra, is the king of the ghosts. Ghostly characters worship Lord Shiva to be gradually guided toward a path of self-realization. Due to grievously sinful acts, such as suicide and causing pain to others, ghosts are bereft of a physical body. Lord Shiva, being merciful, ensures that although such beings are condemned, they get physical bodies.

How merciful, how compassionate he is to be willing to go to the lowest classes of the most sinful people to try to uplift them, even those who are in the darkest regions of the mode of ignorance. That is why he dresses and behaves in such a way as to guide their minds towards the platform of dharma or religious principles. He covers his body with crematorium ashes. He wears venomous snakes on his body. Why? Because he wants to help those persons with such consciousness to identify with him and worship him as their worship-worthy Lord, and uplift them. Therefore, his sacrifice is unparalleled. And it is the sacrifice of pure compassion in his devotion to Lord Krishna.

All human beings have been blessed by the Supreme Lord (Krishna) with a very special facility: the free will to make choices. And when more is given, more is expected out of that. Since we have been given the free will to choose, we are also held responsible for the choices we make. We are expected to behave properly and fulfil the duty of a human being, and that is to purify our existence by acting in line with the will of God and leading a life free from sin. When a human being does the opposite and lives a life of sin by inflicting pain on others, he deserves punishment and must be deprived of the facility given. Such souls are put in the bodies of ghosts. These bodies are constantly afflicted with hunger, thirst and perpetual suffering. Their ability to touch anything and to communicate with anyone is taken away. Moreover, they are unable to initiate any new karma. Instead, they simply experience the consequences of their existing karma. The capacity to enact or amend karma is exclusive to the human form. Sinful souls have no hope of emancipation, and might just continue to feel degraded and suffer eternally. Similar to a person stranded in the middle of the ocean, who cannot escape without assistance from above, sinful souls require the boundless mercy of a higher power to compassionately lift them up. Lord Shiva does that job. He uplifts such downtrodden creatures by his presence and association. And to top it all, he also, at the appropriate time, sends them into human forms, thereby giving them the opportunity to rectify their situation by performing better karmas.

Thus, Lord Shiva provides his association to the ghosts and hobgoblins as an act of his unlimited compassion to elevate them as no one else would do so.

Lord Shiva is like the sun. Suppose a bottle of perfume spills on the street. The sun, through its rays, will make it evaporate and if there is some urine on the street, the sun will make that evaporate as well. But in both instances, the sun remains pure and unaffected. Similarly, Lord Shiva is so powerful that despite associating with such inauspicious beings, he remains pure.

2. Mahajan: The Great Authority

In the Shrimad Bhagavatam (6.3.20–21), Lord Dharmaraj or Yamaraj, the universal judge, describes the names of twelve great personalities who are authorities on the science of God and whose footsteps all beings must follow in order to attain the supreme goal of life:

> *svayambhur naradaa shambhuh*
> *kumarah kapilo manuh*
> *prahlado janako bhishmo*
> *balir vaiyasakir vayam*
> *dvadashaite vijanimo*
> *dharmam bhagavatam bhatah*
> *guhyam vishuddham durbodham*
> *yam jnatvamritam ashnute*

'Lord Brahmā, Bhagavan Narada, Lord Shiva, the four Kumaras, Lord Kapila [the son of Devahuti], Svayambhuva Manu, Prahlada

Maharaj, King Janaka, Grandfather Bhishma,
King Bali, Shukadeva Gosvami and I myself know
the real religious principle. My dear servants,
this transcendental religious principle, which
is known as Bhagavata-dharma, or surrender
unto the Supreme Lord and love for Him, is
uncontaminated by the material modes of nature.
It is very confidential and difficult for
ordinary human beings to understand, but if by
chance one, fortunately, understands it, he is
immediately liberated, and thus he returns
home, back to Godhead.'

Lord Shiva is one of the very few who know the complete
secrets of devotional service to the Supreme Lord. Anyone
who is a sincere follower of Lord Shiva must learn from
his actions and not simply try to imitate him. What Lord
Shiva is teaching his followers is devotional service to the
Supreme Lord. We always see him meditating. That means
there must be an object of meditation. Who is that object?

In his own words, in response to a question posed in
the Padma Purana by Mother Parvati about whose worship
is supreme, Lord Shiva says to the goddess Durga:

aradhananam sarvesham
vishnor aradhanam param
tasmat parataram devi
tadiyanam samarchanam

'My dear Devi, although the Vedas recommend
worship of demigods, the worship of Lord Vishnu

is top-most. However, above the worship of Lord
Vishnu is the rendering of service to Vaishnavas,
who are related to Lord Vishnu.'

In his Ram-Bhujang Stotra (Verse 3), Adi Shankaracharya
(who is the incarnation of Lord Shiva himself) says:

Yadavarnayatkarnamule antakale
shivo rama rameti rameti kashyam |
tadekam param tarakabrahmarupam
bhaje 'ham bhaje 'ham bhaje 'ham bhaje 'ham

'I adore Shri Rama, the greatest one, whose name
is uttered in the ears of the blessed devotees in
Kashi at the time of death by none other than
Lord Shiva Himself. This form/name of the Lord
(Taraka-brahma) is capable of rescuing devotees
from the ocean of samsara.'

So, to be a follower of Lord Shiva is to follow in his
footsteps. To follow in his footsteps does not mean chanting
'*Om namah shivaya*', smoking marijuana or hashish and
drinking bhang. Lord Shiva literally means 'the one who
invokes all auspiciousness' in all directions. How can
intoxicants invoke any auspiciousness? This is not the
mission of Lord Shiva.

But there is not a single reference regarding this in
any scriptures. People have seen the picture of Lord Shiva
sitting down with cupped hands and drinking something
with smoke around him. That is a picture of him drinking
the deadly poison (during the Samudra Manthan) that

was about to destroy all life in the three worlds. But people who want to smoke and want some validation for their habits use this to endorse their sinful habits. If we, for a moment, accept that Lord Shiva smoked, should we also not remember that he drank the ocean of poison too? If anyone wants to imitate one thing, he must be able to duplicate all the other things. If we can drink the ocean of poison, then we have the right to smoke ganja and drink bhang. If we cannot drink the ocean of poison, we should forget imitating him lest we suffer sinful reactions.

People have sinful tendencies and they very conveniently choose what suits their motives. Some unscrupulous people feel that the best way to understand Lord Krishna is to dance with young girls like Lord Krishna did with *gopis*. But Lord Krishna is also Girivaradhari, which means he is the lifter of Govardhan Hill. He also danced on a thousand-hooded snake named Kaliya. So we must first lift Govardhan Hill and dance on at least a single hooded snake (forget thousand-hooded) because He did that before he danced with the gopis. But if we cannot lift Govardhan Hill or dance on a snake, we should forget doing what Lord Krishna did. Instead, follow what He says. Similarly, if we cannot drink the ocean of poison, which invoked the greatest fear even in great demigods like Indra, then we should not try to imitate his other activities. Follow in his footsteps, which means learning what he is trying to teach. Instead of focusing on his external appearance, learn about his internal mood in order to experience the elevation in consciousness and attain the supreme perfection of human life which is God-realization.

3. The Most Compassionate

What is the quality of the greatest personalities which is most perfectly exemplified in the personality of Shankar? What is the most pleasing service to the Supreme Lord that captures His heart? It is the quality of compassion. It is the willingness to make sacrifices for the upliftment of others who have fallen. Lord Shiva is the supreme embodiment of this principle. We find many, many examples in this regard. The Shrimad Bhagavatam (7.10) describes how once the demon Maya attacked all the celestial gods and created three formidable cities that were flying in the air. These cities called the Tripuras, were formidable due to the expert architectural design, and sophisticated defensive and offensive measures used to attack innocent people in the world. Everyone was immensely frustrated. It was Lord Shankar who was called upon by the devotees in great desperation. The Supreme Lord Narayana instructed the devotees to go to Lord Shiva. 'He is the greatest of all. I want him to accomplish the greatest task.' Even though Narayana could have done it himself, He loved to see those whom He loved, get more credit than Him. Just like when Lord Krishna could have killed all the Kurus within one second, but He wanted Arjuna to get the credit.

Lord Shiva with his formidable bows and arrows, destroyed these three cities and thus became known as Tripurari.

The Shrimad Bhagavatam (8.7) describes another glorious pastime of Lord Shiva's most compassionate nature. At the time of the churning of the ocean of milk, the demons and the demigods were on two ends of a mountain

called Mandar. They wanted to churn the ocean in order
to extract nectar. But as they were churning, the first thing
that came out from the ocean was a deadly poison called
Halahala. This poison was so intense and powerful that it
started spreading and growing in all directions. Everyone
understood that it was soon going to destroy all life within
the entire universe and did not know what to do. As usual,
Lord Narayana Himself came to their rescue. As He loves
to glorify His purest and most intimate associates, He led
them all to the holy place known as Kailash, high in the
Himalayas. Once there, all of the devatas began to offer
their prayers of love to Lord Shiva. In a helpless tone, they
said, 'Please Lord Shiva, you are the Supreme Person within
this universe because you are the pure representative of
Narayana Himself. You are manifesting all the divine powers
and potencies of the Supreme Lord by your pure surrender
unto His Lotus Feet, and by your constant meditation of
love. Kindly save us from this imminent destruction that is
upon us.'

At that time, Lord Shiva turned to his wife and spoke:
'My dear Bhavani, just see how all these living entities have
been placed in danger because of the poison produced
from the churning of the ocean of milk. It is my duty to
give protection and safety to all living entities struggling
for existence. Certainly, it is the duty of the master to
protect his suffering dependents. People in general, being
bewildered by the illusory energy of the Supreme Lord, are
always engaged in animosity towards one another. But the
devotees, even at the risk of their own temporary lives, try
to save them.'

He further said in Shrimad Bhagavatam (8.7.40):

> *pumsah kripayato bhadre*
> *sarvatma priyate harih*
> *prite harau bhagavati*
> *priye 'ham sacharacharah*
> *tasmad idam garam bhunje*
> *prajanam svastir astu me*

'My dear gentle wife Bhavani! When one performs
benevolent activities for others, the Supreme
Lord Hari is very pleased. And when the Lord is
pleased, I am also pleased along with all living
creatures. Therefore let me drink this poison for
all the living entities may thus become happy
because of me.'

And thus after informing Bhavani in this way, Lord Shiva
began to drink the poison. The poison had swelled to
become like an ocean. But by his great mystic power, he
concentrated it to fit within the size of the palm of his hand.
We can only imagine the concentrated deadliness of this
poison! And with the spirit of being willing to suffer and
even give up his life in order to show kindness to others, he
took this poison and placed it in his mouth and drank it.

In drinking this poison, Lord Shiva demonstrated the
true quality of how to render the highest service to the
Supreme Lord. As he says in the verse mentioned above,
'pumsah kripayato bhadre, sarvatma priyate harih'—When
one performs benevolent activities for others, the Supreme
Lord Hari is very pleased.

He demonstrated that there is no greater pleasure than being willing to selflessly work, risk one's life and make all sacrifices for the upliftment and welfare of others.

Lord Shiva taught us that a real devotee of the Lord is not concerned with his own happiness and distress. However, he is sensitive toward the happiness and distress of others. And what is the greatest welfare work? To lead a person towards the path of eternal connection with God. And it is not easy. We find throughout the ages, that those personalities who truly dedicate themselves to the highest welfare work of humanity by Lord Krishna's arrangement are often persecuted. Why are they persecuted? It is not by accident or due to some previous bad karma. They are put through hardships and suffering because Lord Krishna wants to show how intensely a devotee is willing to accept any consequences to spread His glories and bring the suffering souls out of their condition of sorrow.

Therefore, those personalities who are in the most loving association with the Lord or want to do the utmost service to please the Lord, are not concerned simply with sitting in a holy place and enjoying the atmosphere. They are willing to risk everything and anything for the purpose of uplifting the world. And Lord Shiva is always engaged in this activity in some capacity or other.

4. The Destroyer

Anything that is material has a shelf life. Matter deteriorates with time. We live in the material world, which, with the passage of time, must come to an end to make way for a fresh start. Creation is exciting and maintenance gives a sense of accomplishment but destruction of something that has been around for a long time is a thankless task.

Lord Shiva carries out this most difficult duty according to the will of Lord Krishna. That is why he is also known as *Mahakal*—the great destroyer.

The material creation consists of countless universes. In each universe, there is a manifestation of Lord Shiva. Each universe has a lifespan which equals the total life span of Lord Brahma i.e. 100 years. But Lord Brahma's 100 years are extensive when translated to earthly calculations. In the universe we currently live in, Lord Brahma's 100 years are equivalent to 311.04 trillion years. When it is time for the universe to end, Lord Shiva does his tandav dance and destroys everything. However, he is not alone in this task.

The Brahma Purana (124.24–28) elaborates that by employing the flames from the divine serpent Sheshanaga or Anantashesha (Lord Sankarshana), the Supreme burns the nether worlds from below. This fire of universal destruction reaches the earth and burns the entire surface along with the Bhuvah and Svarga worlds (the higher planets). When the higher planets are set on fire, the residents leave their subtle bodies for Maharloka.[54] However, as explained in the Brahmanda Purana (3.4.1.157), the fires of devastation move throughout the universe and this time, in the final annihilation of the cosmos, burn the celestial planets, such as the Bhuvaloka, Bhuvarloka and Svarloka worlds, as well as the Maharloka planetary system. Elsewhere in the Bhagavatam (5.25.3), it states that Lord Shiva plays a significant role in the final annihilation of the universe: 'At the time of devastation, when Lord Anantadeva [Ananta Sesha, Sankarshana] desires to destroy the entire creation, He becomes slightly angry. Then, from between

---

[54] A heavenly planet.

His two eyebrows appears three-eyed Rudra, carrying a trident. This Rudra, who is known as Sankarshana, is the embodiment of the eleven Rudras, or incarnations of Lord Shiva within the universe. He appears in order to devastate the entire creation.'

The Brahma Purana (124.16) explains that it is the imperishable Lord Krishna who assumes the form of Rudra to bring all the elements and living beings back into Himself in the process of annihilation.

After Lord Shiva appears, he begins to do his dance of dissolution wildly to the beat of his drum. 'At the time of dissolution, Lord Shiva's hair is scattered, and he pierces the rulers of the different directions with his trident. He laughs and dances proudly, scattering their hands like flags, as thunder scatters the clouds all over the world.'[55] Lord Shiva's dancing causes such a commotion that it brings in the clouds, which cause the universe to become inundated with water.

5. The Bhakti Yoga Teacher

There are four Vaishnava *Sampradayas*, authorized by the Supreme Lord to distribute the Vedic knowledge about Him in this world. The word 'sampradaya' is a passive nominal formation from the Sanskrit verb root, sam-pra-da ('to hand down').

Without being carefully handed down in a proper sampradaya, no knowledge can be authentic.

The Padma Purana states:

---

[55] Shrimad Bhagavata 4.5.10

sampradaya-vihina ye mantras te nisphala matah
atah kalau bhavisyanti catvarah sampradayinah
sri-brahma-rudra-sanakah vaisnavah ksiti-
pavanah catvaras te kalau bhavya hy utkale
purusottamat

'Any mantra that does not come in disciplic succession is considered to be fruitless. Therefore, four divine individuals will appear in the age of Kali to found disciplic schools. The founders of these four Vaishnava sampradayas are Lakshmi or Shri, Brahma, Rudra and Sanaka Rishi, and the acharyas of the Kali Age who follow their lines will appear in the holy city of Purusottama in Orissa.'

Further, it is stated in Prameya-ratnavali (1.7):

ramanujam shrih svichakre madhvacharyam
chaturmukhah shri-vishnu-svaminam rudro
nimbadityam chatuhsanah

'Lakshmi accepted Ramanujacarya as her representative; Lord Brahma selected Madhvacharya. Lord Shiva chose Vishnu Swami and the four Kumaras, Nimbarkacharya.'

An important point to note here is that one of the four disciplic lines, Rudra Sampradaya, is headed by Lord Shiva personally. And it is a Vaishnava Sampradaya, which means that it propagates devotion to Lord Krishna or Lord Vishnu.

Lord Shiva chose the great Vishnu Swami as his representative to teach bhakti to Lord Krishna in Kaliyuga. At present, the famous Pustimarg sampradaya, founded by Shri Vallabhacharya, represents the Rudra Sampradaya. Thus, Lord Shiva, along with playing the role of the administrator of the Universe, also preaches bhakti yoga—devotional service to Lord Krishna.

6. The Greatest Vaishnav

The Supreme Lord has a will and a plan. He uses His most surrendered devotee to execute that plan. A real devotee only focuses on carrying out the instructions of the Lord without caring for personal happiness. He does what makes the Lord happy. The greatest scripture Shrimad Bhagavatam (12.13.16) describes Lord Shiva as the greatest devotee of Vaishnav:

> *nimna-ganam yatha ganga*
> *devanam achyuto yatha*
> *vaishnavanam yatha shambhuh*
> *purananam idam tatha*

'Just as the Ganga is the greatest of all rivers, Lord Achyuta [Lord Krishna] the supreme among deities and Lord Shambhu [Shiva] the greatest of Vaishnavas, so Shrimad-Bhagavatam is the greatest of all Puranas.'

Lord Shiva is entrusted with the most difficult tasks. The greatest pleasure of a devotee is to glorify His Lord and engage as many people as possible to His lotus feet. This activity is the life and soul of any Vaishnav.

But what if a devotee has to do the opposite—lead people away from the Lord's devotional service? Even though a devotee would rather die than do this, Lord Krishna sometimes wants this to be done to segregate real devotees from pseudo-ones. Such people only cause disturbance to the Lord and confusion to people in general.

The test is a simple one: when something cheap is thrown, pseudo devotees will enthusiastically pick it up, whereas the real devotees will only accept the essence.

About 1500 years ago, Lord Shiva appeared as the great Shankaracharya and propagated a dubious philosophy of *Mayavad*, which essentially taught that the Supreme Lord is formless and His form is just an illusion (*maya*). He claimed that the goal of life was to become one with Him. It is a painful philosophy for a genuine devotee because by negating the form of the Lord, it also negates the opportunity of service to the Lord, and for a devotee, serving the Lord is his life and soul. And how painful it must have been for the greatest devotee Lord Shiva to misguide people? But he did it successfully. Towards the end of his life, he did reveal his heart and instructed his followers to only worship Shankaracharya in his famous composition says:

bhaja govindam bhaja govindam
govindamm bhajamudhamate
samprapte sannihite kale
nahi nahi rakshati

'Worship Govinda, Worship Govinda, Worship
Govinda. Oh fool! Rules of grammar will not save
you at the time of your death.'

bhaja govindam bhaja govindam
govindam bhajamūudhamate
nama smarana danyam upayam
nahi pashyamo bhavatarane

'Worship Govinda, worship Govinda, worship
Govinda, Oh fool! Other than chanting the Lord's
names, there is no other way to cross life's ocean.'

Lord Shiva had revealed his heart much before his advent
in this world. In Padma Purana (6.236.7–11), he said:

mayavadam asac chastram pracchannam
bauddham uchyate
mayaiva kalpitam devi kalau brahmana-rupina
brahmanash chaparam rupam nirgunam
vakshyate maya
sarva-svam jagato 'py asya mohanartham
kalau yuge
vedante tu maha-shastre mayavadam avaidikam
mayaiva vakshyate devi jagatam nasha-karanat

'"The Mayavada philosophy," Lord Shiva
informed his wife Parvati, "is impious. It is
closet Buddhism or atheism. My dear Parvati, in
Kaliyuga, I assume the form of a brahmana and

teach this imagined Mayavada philosophy. In order to cheat the atheists, I describe the Supreme Lord to be without form and qualities. Similarly, while explaining Vedanta, I describe the same Mayavada philosophy in order to mislead the entire population toward atheism by denying the personal form of the Lord.'

In the Shiva Purana, the Supreme Lord told Lord Shiva:

dvaparadau yuge bhutva kalaya manushadishu svagamaih kalpitais tvam ca janan mad-vimukhan kuru

'In Kaliyuga, mislead the people in general by propounding imaginary meanings for the Vedas to bewilder them.'

These are the descriptions in the Puranas that act as evidence of Lord Shiva taking up the most arduous task on the instruction of the Supreme Lord Vishnu, the maintainer of the universe.

Thus, Lord Shiva acts as a perfect teacher for all devotees of Lord Krishna/Lord Vishnu, and teaches by his example, the limits of complete surrender i.e. the hallmark quality of a real devotee of the Lord.

7. The Gunavatar

There are primarily six categories of avatars (incarnations) of the Supreme Lord Shri Krishna:

(a) Purusha Avatars:
Lord Mahavishnu: in charge of creating the material universes and the ingredients required for further creation.
Garbodhakshayi Vishnu: gives birth to Lord Brahma in each universe.
Ksirodakshayi Vishnu: in charge of the maintenance of the universe.

(b) Lila Avatars: Matsya, Kurma, Narasimha, Ram and others who incarnate from time to time to perform beautiful pastimes.

(c) Shaktyavesh Avatars: a living entity empowered by the Lord to execute His mission. Example: Lord Parashurama, Narada and Sage Vyasa.

(d) Manavantra Avatars: appearing during the reign of Manu, the father of mankind, to help run the universe.

(e) Yuga Avatars: appear in every yuga to propagate the spiritual practice meant for the particular yuga.

(f) Guna Avatars: in charge of managing the three gunas or modes of material nature, namely, mode of goodness, mode of passion and mode of ignorance.

Lord Shiva is in charge of the mode of ignorance.
The material creation in which we live is predominated by the three modes: mode of goodness, mode of passion and mode of ignorance. Everything in the world—the food

we eat, the music we listen to, the bodies we have, the places, the actions—falls under these three gunas or modes.

To simplify it further, let us take the example of a city where everything, including the roads, hospitals, different areas, restaurants and gardens fall under some department that manages them. Anything anyone does in a particular area/field, will be overseen by the corresponding department associated with the act. So, the three modes can be considered the three department heads active within the material world.

Every time we make a choice, we become conditioned by that mode. Suppose we like a particular type of food. Since it will fall under one of the three modes, we become conditioned by that mode. The more we make a choice, the stronger the conditioning of the particular mode becomes. Depending on which of the three modes controls us the most, we take birth in a particular body and family, or have a personality with a set of likes and dislikes. Out of the three, the mode of goodness is the best as it is characterized by a sense of happiness, clarity to make the right choices and freedom from sin. The mode of passion is intermediate, but the mode of ignorance is considered the lowest, in which a person is devoid of a sense of discrimination and his happiness comes from acts which are sinful. Such people have no hope and enter miserable conditions of existence, and need to be uplifted.

The most compassionate Lord Shiva, as Gunavatar, in charge of those in ignorance, takes control of such living entities and by his association, purifies them and elevates them. This is also the reason he dresses up in a particular way to attract beings living in crematoriums—with ashes all over his body, matted hair, apparently unclean; typical of those in the mode of ignorance. Thus, such living entities are easily able to relate to him and come near him, getting a chance to be elevated in their consciousness to the mode of goodness.

This is the reason Lord Shiva is also revered by the devotees of Lord Krishna, among his many roles, as the greatest Vaishnava. He has limitless empathy for those who have no shelter.

But while he associates with the mode of ignorance, we must always remember that he remains unaffected by its influence. He is always situated in pure goodness due to his constant mediation on his deity Lord Sankarshana and thus, teaches us an extremely valuable lesson: no matter where we are or what mode we are in, if we keep our mind fixed on the Supreme Lord Krishna/Narayana, we shall also remain unaffected by the material influences (anger, greed, selfishness, envy etc.). We remain like a lotus leaf, which is surrounded by water but not even a drop can stay on it.

Chapter 16

History of the Twelve Jyotirlingas

A 'lingam' means a symbolic representation of Lord Shiva and a jyotirliga means 'the radiant sign of Lord Shiva'.

There were originally sixty-four jyotirlingas, out of which twelve are considered to be highly auspicious and holy. Each considered a different manifestation of Lord Shiva, these are, since ancient times, the prime places of worship for the devotees of Lord Shiva.

The distribution of twelve jyotirlinga temples is as follows:

Two jyotirlingas are on the sea shore.
Three jyotirlingas are on river banks.
Four jyotirlingas are in the heights of the mountains.
Three jyotirlingas are in the villages located in meadows.

1. Somnath

Lord Brahma is the secondary creator within the universe, and upon the order of Lord Vishnu, he is entrusted with the responsibility of bringing various living entities into this world according to their karmas. To accomplish this task, he created a race of progenitors called the 'Prajapatis', who further helped in giving birth to various living entities as a part of the process of creation. The most prominent of these progenitors was Daksha. He was extremely powerful, famous and effulgent. He had twenty-seven daughters, all of whom were given in marriage to the moon god, Som. Gaining the charming and effulgent moon god as their husband, the daughters of Daksha felt extremely fortunate and appeared even more beautiful, and the moon god shone even brighter after getting such beautiful wives.

However, as time passed, Som became exceedingly attached to just one wife, Rohini, and neglected the others. This deeply pained the other wives, who went to their father Daksha and related their pitiable condition. Listening to them, Daksha also became morose and his effulgent face became discoloured like a leaf burnt in a forest fire. In an attempt to help his daughters and rectify Somdev's partial behaviour, Daksha went to Som and requested him: 'You are born in a pure and respected family lineage. Why are you thinking less of the girls who are living under your shelter? Why are you nice to one and neglectful of others? Whatever has happened, has happened till now but please be careful in the future as such partial behaviour leads a person to hell.'

After humbly requesting this from his son-in-law, Daksha went back home convinced that Somdev would not repeat his mistake. However, Somdev did not heed his request and became so attached to Rohini that he did not respect his other wives. When Daksha heard this again, he was extremely broken-hearted and decided to try and speak to Somdev one last time. However, Somdev was extremely casual about the situation, which infuriated Daksha even more. Seeing no other way to bring Somdev to his senses, Daksha cursed him to be infected with a deadly disease called tuberculosis (TB). The moon plays an important role in sustaining life in the universe, and when he became weak due to disease and his moonbeams lost their effulgence, chaos arose in the three worlds. All the sages and celestial gods were in shock. 'Alas! Alas! How will Somdev get cured?' they cried. There was a state of confusion among everyone as they didn't know what to do. Somdev related his calamitous condition to Indra, the king of the heavens and the celestial sages. Seeing no other recourse, they went to seek shelter from Lord Brahma.

Lord Brahma, after hearing their plea, advised, 'Forget whatever has happened. The curse cannot be reversed, but a solution that I suggest can certainly end it.'

He continued, 'Listen very carefully! Along with all the celestial Gods, Somdev should go to the sacred place named Prabhas, and there, he should chant the Mahamrityunjay mantra and worship Lord Shiva. He should install a shivaling and perform austerities for the pleasure of Lord Shiva, who is Ashutosh (the one who is easily pleased). Being pleased with Somdev, Lord Shiva will certainly free him from his disease.'

Under the guidance and instructions of the great sages and the celestial Gods, Somdev performed severe austerities and worshipped Lord Shiva by chanting 10 crore Mahamrityunjay mantras in Prabhas for six months. Chanting the mantra and meditating on Lord Shiva, Somdev stood in one spot with great determination.

Seeing his severe penance, Lord Shiva, extremely pleased, appeared in front of Somdev and said, 'Dear Somdev! Please ask whatever your heart desires. I am extremely pleased with you. I shall grant you the best of boons.'

In deep gratitude, Somdev spoke, 'Dear Lord! If you are pleased with me, what is impossible for me to achieve? Please free me from this disease and forgive me for the offence that I have committed.'

Lord Shiva replied, 'I bless you that one fortnight, your phases will decrease but the other fortnight, you will enjoy a continuous increase.'

Gaining this much relief, a delighted Som worshipped Lord Shiva and offered the choicest of prayers in his glorification.

Lord Shiva, being very pleased with all the celestial Gods and wanting to increase the fame of Prabhas *kshetra*[56] and that of Somdev, made the shivaling installed by Somdev famous in the three worlds as 'Somnath' or 'Someshewar'.

According to Shiva Purana, by worshipping the Somnath Jyotirlinga, a person can easily become free from diseases such as TB or leprosy.

Somdev is glorious due to his austerities, caused by which, the most merciful Lord Shiva became eternally situated at Prabhas to shower his grace on everyone for all time to come.

---

[56] Area.

The celestial gods, being ecstatic at the mercy shown to Somdev, created a small pond and named it 'Somkund'. The Shiva Purana states that Lord Shiva and Lord Brahma always reside within this pond, and anyone who bathes in this pond becomes free from all sins. Incurable diseases such as TB easily get cured by bathing in this pond for six months. Every desire gets fulfilled in this sacred place.

After being blessed by the most merciful Lord Shiva, Somdev, the moon god, resumed his duties as before.

Anyone who listens or makes other listen to this pastime of the appearance of Somnath Jyotirlinga, will have all his desires fulfilled and become free from all sins.

This jyotirlinga, located in the vibrant state of Gujarat, is one of the twelve prominent jyotirlingas of Lord Shiva in India. Revered for its religious significance, the temple has been a pilgrimage site for centuries and is renowned for its architectural beauty. It stands as a testament to the undying faith and devotion of its devotees, having been rebuilt several times after being destroyed (starting in the year 1026 by Mahmud of Ghazni, 1299 by Ulugh Khan, 1395 by Muzaffar Shah I and 1669 by Aurangzeb). With a backdrop of the vast Arabian Sea, the serene ambience of Somnath offers a divine and tranquil experience to pilgrims and tourists alike.

Timings: The temple is generally open from 6 a.m. to 9 p.m. However, specific rituals and aarti timings can vary, so it's advisable to check the temple's official website or contact the temple authorities before planning a visit.

How to Reach: Somnath has its railway station and is well-connected to major cities of India. Regular bus services connect Somnath to various cities in Gujarat. Additionally, the state's extensive road network makes it convenient for visitors to drive to Somnath or hire taxis from major cities like Ahmedabad or Rajkot.

2. Mallikarjuna

Lord Shiva and Mother Parvati were very happy relishing the childhood of their two sons—Lord Ganesh and Kartikeya. Seeing their children play, Lord Shiva's and Mother Parvati's affection for their sons grew day by day just like the phases of the moon. Lord Ganesh and Kartikeya also, through their respectful and helpful attitude, won the hearts of their parents.

One day, as Lord Shiva and Mother Parvati were peacefully seated in seclusion, they started discussing: 'Both our children are grown up now. We must get them married. But to whom and how? We love both our children equally.' Thinking about this, they went into deep thought with transcendental anxiety.

Meanwhile, when Lord Ganesh and Kartikeya came to know of their parents' plans for their marriage, both started debating as to who would get married first. Lord Ganesh wanted to marry first, but Kartikeya argued that he should marry before Lord Ganesh.

Lord Shiva and Mother Parvati were bewildered when they saw their children behaving this way. After some time, they called both their sons and told them: 'We have already made a rule for your marriage, which would be beneficial for both of you. Since we love both of you equally, we cannot be siding with one and neglecting the other. Therefore, for your welfare and to keep things impartial, we are putting forward a condition for your marriage. Whoever completes the *parikrama*[57] of the Earth first, will get to marry first.'

As soon as the mighty Kartikeya heard the condition, he left to complete the task without wasting a single moment. However, the supremely intelligent Lord Ganesh did not move. He thought, 'What do I do now? Certainly, I cannot complete this difficult task. I get tired walking a few miles, so how could I possibly cover the earth?'

After indulging in deep thought, he quietly left and returned after taking a bath. He laid down two seats and requested Lord Shiva and Mother Parvati to kindly sit on them and fulfil his heart's desire. The parents happily complied.

Lord Ganesh then diligently worshipped them according to the proper procedure using the best of paraphernalia. He circumambulated them seven times and offered beautiful prayers in their glorification.

After completing his worship, Lord Ganesh requested his illustrious parents, 'Now please get me married without delay.'

Lord Shiva and Mother Parvati were astonished and said, 'Dear son! We shall certainly get you married. But first, please go and fulfil the condition. Circumambulate the earth and return before your brother who has already left.'

Lord Ganesh got visibly upset and replied, 'Both of you are supremely elevated, extremely intelligent and hyper-aware of religious principles. How can you still talk like this?'

---

[57] Circumambulation.

'Not once but seven times I have circumambulated the earth and sufficiently fulfilled the condition.'

Lord Shiva and Mother Parvati asked in surprise, 'This mighty earth is covered with vast oceans! When did you circumambulate it? What are you up to?'

The most intelligent Lord Ganesh clarified: 'My dear father and mother, I have, with utmost care, worshipped and circumambulated both of you. Thus, I have already circumambulated the earth.' He continued, 'Correct me if I am wrong. The Vedas and other scriptures emphatically declare that by duly worshipping and circumambulating the parents, one gets the benefit of circumambulating the entire earth. And I have done that not once but seven times. Now tell me if this is not true. Either accept what I am presenting and marry me off or proclaim that the Vedas are false [which is impossible as they are the words of God].'

Lord Shiva and Mother Parvati were impressed. They could not refute what Lord Ganesh said. 'Whatever he has presented is absolutely correct,' they thought.

They praised Lord Ganesh for his incomparable intelligence and agreed to marry him off. Soon, they got him married to Riddhi and Siddhi, the two daughters of the great King Prajapati Vishwarup.

Lord Ganesh lived happily and in due course, became father to two illustrious sons—Kshem (born of Riddhi) and Laabh (born of Siddhi).

One fine day, Kartikeya returned home after duly fulfilling the condition of circumambulating the Earth. When Narada informed him of all the events that took place in his absence, he felt extremely upset and disappointed. In his anger, he immediately, left home and went to Kraunch mountain. Lord Shiva and Mother Parvati were heartbroken upon hearing this news, and came to Kraunch mountain to bring him home. But when Kartikeya heard about them coming, he went farther away. Not willing to bear the separation from their son, both Lord Shiva and Mother Parvati decided to stay there and manifested as a jyotirlinga, which became famous by the name 'Mallikarjun' (Mallika refers to Mother Parvati and Arjun is another name for Lord Shiva). Thus, both are present in this one jyotirlinga, giving it a unique presence among all jyotirlingas. Eager to see their child out of parental affection, both Lord Shiva and Mother Parvati go to see their son on the festival days. Lord Shiva goes on *amavasya*[58] and Mother Parvati goes on *poornima*.[59]

Whoever takes darshan of this jyotirlinga becomes free from all sinful reactions and gets all his desires fulfilled.

Mallikarjuna jyotirlinga, also known as Srisailam temple, is situated in the picturesque landscapes of the Nallamala Hills in Andhra Pradesh. Revered as one of the twelve sacred jyotirlingas of Lord Shiva, it stands alongside the temple of Goddess Bhramaramba, making the site doubly auspicious. Rich in history and religious significance, Mallikarjuna is not only a focal point for Lord Shiva devotees but also an architectural marvel, reflecting the grandeur of ancient Indian temple art. Along with its spiritual ambience, the temple's location offers a serene escape amidst dense forests and the winding Lord Krishna River.

---

[58] New moon day.

[59] Full moon day.

Timings: The temple is usually open from 5 a.m. to 3.30 p.m. and then from 6 p.m. to 10 p.m. It's advisable to check the temple's official website or get in touch with local authorities for any changes in timings or special events.

How to Reach: The closest railway station is Markapur, situated around 85 km from Shrisailam. Buses and taxis are available from the station to the temple. Shrisailam is well-connected by road—state-run buses from major towns and cities in Andhra Pradesh, like Hyderabad, Tirupati and Vijayawada, frequently ply to Shrisailam. The road journey offers scenic views of the Nallamala forest range as well.

3. Mahakaleshwar

In the holy city of Avanti (present-day Ujjain) which awards liberation to one and all, and which is extremely dear to Lord Shiva, there lived a pious and religious Brahmana named Vedapriya. True to his name, he was extremely dedicated to the Vedic culture. Every day, he would perform *agnihotra* yajna[60] at home and was always engaged in worshipping Lord Shiva with utmost care and devotion. Lord Shiva was his life and soul. The Brahmana would make a shivaling out of the earth and offer elaborate worship as per the prescribed methods. Whenever he was not worshipping his Lord, he was busy studying the scriptures, thus bathing himself in the nectar of divine knowledge. Due to his complete dedication to the spiritual culture, even though he lived a family life, he had attained a state of being that was only attainable by saintly people.

---

[60] A Vedic ritual of offering ghee into sacred fire along with chanting of mantras.

The Brahmana had four equally qualified sons—Devapriya, Priyamedha, Sukrit and Suvrat. Because of the presence of this illustrious family in Avanti, the glory and fame of the city increased day by day and it became radiant.

At the same time, on a mountain named Ratnamal, a demon named Dushan performed severe austerities and gained tremendous powers from Lord Brahma. As is the nature of the demons, as soon as they get some power, they take to the destruction of the innocent. True to his nature, the demon sent his armies to destroy all the pious followers of the Vedic dharma. Eventually, he also attacked the brahmanas of Avanti. Using his mystic powers, he produced four fierce demons who appeared like the fire of devastation. Everyone started running for their lives, but Vedapriya and his family remained unperturbed. They encouraged everyone to not be afraid and instead have faith in the most compassionate Lord Shiva. Saying this, all of them sat down in front of the shivaling to invoke Lord Shiva's protection.

When Dushan saw these brahmanas engaged in the worship of their deity, he came running and shouted, 'Kill them! Kill them!' However, the sons of Vedapriya did not pay any attention to him as they were deeply engrossed in remembering Lord Shiva. As soon as the demons came close to killing them, there was an explosion. A big hole appeared right at the spot where the sons of Vedapriya had installed the shivaling. From the hole appeared the most ferocious form of Lord Shiva, trident in hand, as the great destroyer, Mahakal!

Lord Shiva angrily addressed the demons, 'You rascals! Just to destroy devils like you, I have appeared as Mahakal (the Lord of Death, Kaal, is symbolic of death). Get away from these pious brahmanas.' Saying this, the Lord, simply with his powerful roar, turned Dushan and his fellow demons to ashes in an instant. Whoever was left in the army, ran away.

The celestial Gods played drums and showered flowers upon the Lord in celebration of his victory.

Since Lord Shiva was extremely pleased with the worship of Vedapriya's sons, he told them to ask for a boon.

The four brothers, in deep gratitiude, with their heads bowed down in respect, spoke, 'Dear Lord! Please bless us with liberation from this material word. For the benefit of all people, the present and the ones to come in future, please stay here in this very place. Please give those who come on pilgrimage here moksha.'

Lord Shiva, who is extremely merciful, happily accepted their request and a jyotirlinga was installed in the place where he first appeared. This fierce form of his is known as Mahakal or Mahakaleshwar since he came as the Lord of Death. This is the reason why the deity in this temple is facing south, unlike all other temples. It is said that only in death one faces south and the abode of Yamaraj, the Lord of Death, is also in the south. It is as if Lord Shiva is loudly proclaiming that he will send anyone who tries to trouble his devotees to the abode of death in the south.

Anyone who sees this jyotirlinga will not experience any misery even in his dreams. Anyone who worships this jyotirlinga with whatever desire in their mind will certainly have it fulfilled and attain Shivaloka as his destination in the end.

Location: The temple is located in the historical city of Ujjain in Madhya Pradesh, India. It is situated on the banks of the holy river, Shipra.

Timings: Every day, 4 a.m. to 11 p.m.

Nearest railway station: Ujjain Junction

4. Omkareshwar

Once, after having offered his prayers to Lord Shiva at a holy place called Gokarna (in present-day Karnataka), the great sage Narada Muni went to meet King Vindhyachal, the person in charge of the Vindhyachal mountain. Vindhayachal, feeling extremely delighted at the arrival of the most revered guest, received him with the utmost respect and offered him a nice place to sit. However, there was a problem. Vindhyachal had developed some subtle pride in his position. He told Narada Muni, 'I have got the best of everything and never face any shortage in my kingdom.'

Narad Muni, sensing this false pride, desired to cure this deadly disease. In his own mysterious yet seemingly amusing manner, he told Vindhyachal, 'You know what? You are certainly very great and powerful, and you are the embodiment of all other mountains. But Mount Sumeru seems to have its special place and fame within this universe. Although you have all the qualities desirable in a person, still you are no match for Sumeru. Have you seen the size of Sumeru? His peaks are so high that they are touching the higher planets of the celestial Gods. You can never reach so high.'

Hearing Narada's words, Vindhyachal felt extremely sad. He began to think, 'My life is useless. I am good for nothing. When I am of no use to anyone, I must do something to improve my life.' Determined to do something about the situation, he resolved to seek Lord Shiva's blessings and came to Omkar mountain. After making a shivaling out of earth, he started worshipping the Lord with the proper procedure. For hours, he sat deeply immersed in meditation on the lotus feet of Lord Shiva. His austerities continued for six months. He worshipped Lord Shiva with such focus that for these six months, he did not even move from his prayer mat. One day, pleased with his dedicated penance, Lord Shiva appeared in front of Vindhyachal and asked him to request a boon.

Vindhyachal, overwhelmed seeing the object of his worship, fell at Lord Shiva's feet and said, 'My dear Lord! If you are pleased with me, then please bless me with the right intelligence. Please rectify my wrong mentality. Help me with intelligence so I can use it to accomplish what is in my heart.'

Lord Shiva happily consented and blessed, 'So be it!'

Right at this moment, the great, pure-hearted sages and celestial Gods appeared and requested Lord Shiva to permanently stay at this place. The Lord happily accepted their request and manifested himself as a jyotirlinga, which came to be known as Omkareshwar. However, at the behest of the sages and the celestials, Lord Shiva split the linga into two parts—one stayed on the Omkar mountain as Omkareshwar and the other one, the earthly shivaling (made by King Vindhya) in which the light (*jyoti*) from the Omkareshwar Jyotirlinga entered, became famous as Amareshwar or Mamleshwar.

All the assembled sages and celestial gods duly worshipped both the lingas and received numerous boons from Lord Shiva for pleasing him. Thereafter, all of them returned to their respective abodes and King Vindhyachal also gave up his lamentation.

Both Omkareshwar and Mamleshwar are similar to each other. Thus, pilgrims throughout the year take great pleasure in visiting both holy sites next to each other.

Mamleshwar Jyotirlinga is on the south bank of the sacred river Narmada, and Omkareshwar Jyotirlinga sits on the Omkar mountain towards the north bank of the Narmada. Narmada is in the middle of both temples.

One legend says that two sons of emperor Mandhata, King Ambarish and King Mucchkund of the Ikshvaku dynasty, performed severe austerities and pleased Lord Shiva, because of which this mountain (on which Omkareshwar is situated) is also called Mandhata Mountain. Since Lord Shiva manifested himself as a jyotirlinga here, it is also known as Mandhata Omkareshwar.

The island on which the Omkareshwar Island is situated is in the shape of a revered Vedic symbol, hence the name Omkar Mountain.

Location: Mandhata, Madhya Pradesh
Timings: Every day from 5 a.m. to 10 p.m.
Nearest Railway Station: Omkareshwar Road

5. Kedarnath

After the Battle of Kurukshetra, the Pandavas went to see Lord Shiva in Kashi to atone for the killing of so many of their kinsmen in battle. When Lord Shiva learned that the Pandavas were coming, he fled and playfully hid from them. The Pandavas discovered Lord Shiva in the Himalayas, in a place called Gupta Kashi ('Hidden Kashi'), where he had disguised himself as a brahmana. Having been identified, Lord Shiva ran away to a valley and disguised himself as a bull, but Bhima recognized him. Bhima stretched his big legs from one end of the valley to the other and caught the bull by its tail. Lord Shiva, still trying to hide, began to bury himself in the ground. But the determination of the Pandavas won him over, and before the bull's hump had disappeared, he decided to give them an audience.

Lord Shiva instructed the Pandavas to worship the hump of the bull. That is why the shape of this jyotirlinga is different from the others as it appears in the shape of a hump. This jyotirlinga became famous as Kedareshwar or Kedarnath Jyotirlinga since it is situated in the area known as Kedar, in front of Kedar Mountain. The Pandavas built a nice temple and the worship they started is still going on. Other parts of Lord Shiva's body appeared in other mountains, and the Pandavas also built temples there. They are known as *Panch Kedars* (five Kedars): (1) Kedarnath—hump, (2) Tuganath—arm, (3) Rudranath—face, (4) Kalpeshwar—hair and (5) Madhyamaheswar—navel.

They are at altitudes ranging from 1500 to 3680 m. It takes about fourteen days to visit all the five places. They can all be reached by a long circular trek.

Another legend has it that the supreme Lord Narayan appeared in a humanlike pastime with his dear associate and friend Nara (Arjun), and performed austerities in Badrinath. Since Lord Narayan and Lord Shiva cannot stay away from each other, upon the sages Nara–Narayan's request, Lord Shiva decided to manifest in the Kedar area as a lingam, which became famous as Kedarnath.

Location: Uttarakhand
Time to visit: May to June

The temple opens in the first week of May and closes either the last week of October or the first week of November. May/June is the busiest time of the year. Worship is continued in the village of Okhimath in the winter by the priest from the Kedarnath Temple. The waiting time to enter the temple in the afternoon is about fifteen minutes. If you go at 7 a.m., the waiting time may be two hours or more. The main worship is at 6 a.m. and 6 p.m.

Visiting the Panch Kedars

We could start at Kedarnath, return to Guptakashi, go to Okhimath and continue to Mansuna village. From Mansuna village, it is a 24 km-trek to Madhyamaheswar. You could stay at Ransi overnight, proceed to Gondhar (3 km) and climb 10 km to Madhyamaheswar. The temple here is a small stone temple dedicated to the middle (*madhya*) part of the bull-Shiva. Hence, the name 'Madhyamaheswar'.

Tungnath (12,065 ft) is the highest (in altitude) temple in India. It is surrounded by striking mountains, such as Neelkanth, Kedarnath and Nanda Devi. The Lord Shiva temple here is on a stone-paved platform overlooking a cliff. Tungnath represents the arm of Lord Shiva. There are five silver images, representing the faces of the Pandavas along with images representing Sage Vyasa and Kalabhairava in the temple. There is also a small Parvati temple here. We can get to this place by trekking from Chopta (7km, 4 hr), which is 37 km from Okhimath.

To get to Kalpeshwar Temple, we first need to take a bus to Helang village, which is 14 km south of Joshimath (another famous site in the area). From Helang, we walk for 9 km to the village named Urgam. From Urgam, it is a 1.5 km walk to Kalpeshwar Temple.

Next, we reach Gopeshwar by road and proceed to Sagar, followed by a 24 km trek to Rudranath. To get to Rudranath, we can also trek from Kalpeshwar. Rudraganga flows by the Rudranath temple and there are breathtaking views of the Trishul, Nanda Devi and Parbat peaks.

6. Bhimashankar

Once upon a time on the Sahyadri mountain, there lived a mighty demon called Bhima. He was living with his mother Karkati, and true to his nature, he would take great pleasure in going against dharma (righteousness). He went out of his way to cause pain to others, especially to those who followed the path of dharma.

One day, out of great curiosity, he approached his mother and enquired, 'Dear Mother! Please tell me who my father is. Why do you live alone on this mountain? I want to know everything.'

Karkati replied, 'Your father was Kumbhkarna, the mighty brother of the powerful Ravana. But both of them were killed by Lord Ram. My husband was Viradh, who was also killed by Ram. My parents were Karkat and Pushkasi. One day, they went in search of food and attacked Sutiskhna, the glorious disciple of the great sage Agastya, with the intention of devouring him. But Sutishkna, with his mystic powers, killed my parents. Since all my protectors were gone, I started living alone on this mountain. However, one day the demon Kumbhkarna came here and saw that I was alone. He forced himself upon me and then left. In due course of time, you were born. Thus I have been living here alone with you as my only hope and shelter.'

Bhima turned furious upon hearing that both his father and Viradha, his mother's protector, were killed by Lord Vishnu. Not only that, his grandparents also died at the hands of Lord Vishnu's devotee (Sutishkna). Vowing to take revenge, he performed severe austerities for 1000 years to please Lord Brahma. Pleased with him, Lord Brahma finally appeared and granted him invincible powers.

Proudly, Bhima promised his mother that he would destroy Lord Vishnu and all his associates. He attacked the heavens and drove all, including Lord Indra and other celestial Gods who are Lord Vishnu's servants, out of their celestial kingdom. After gaining control of the heavens, he set his eyes on Earth and attacked the kingdom of Kamrup ruled by the devoted King Sudakshina. A great battle ensued in which Sudakshina was defeated and captured by Bhima. He was imprisoned with his legs tied up in heavy chains. However, since Sudakshina was devoted to Lord Shiva, even inside the prison his devotion did not waver, and he continued to offer his daily prayers to his deity by making a shivaling out of earth.

Meanwhile, the demon Bhima became even more vengeful as he increased his atrocities and destroyed everyone who followed the path of the Vedas, the word of God.

Deeply saddened by this, Indra and the other celestial Gods prayed to Lord Shiva to protect them from this catastrophe. Lord Shiva consented but told them to first give a special message to his dear devotee Sudakshina who was devotedly engaged in his service even inside the prison.

Lord Shiva said, 'Please tell Sudakshina to deeply meditate on me with love and I shall soon put an end to this demon's cruelty.'

The sages and the celestial deities happily delivered the message to the King in the prison, who was overjoyed to receive this special blessing from his Lord. As per the instruction of the Lord, Sudakshina intensified his meditation on Lord Shiva and stayed immersed in his practice for long hours.

Unknown to everyone including the King, Lord Shiva and Mother Parvati came to the prison and started residing with the King.

When the guards saw the King suddenly become so deeply engrossed in his worship in contrast to the previous days, they were alarmed and hurriedly went to inform their master that Sudakshina was engaged in some special ritual that seemed to be intended to kill him. Enraged, the demon Bhima came charging with sword in hand, and burst into anger upon seeing the King and various articles of worship strewn all around. Seeing this, he was fully convinced that the King was planning to kill him. In retaliation, he picked up his sword and attacked the shivaling that the King used to worship. But even before the sword could touch the shivaling, Lord Shiva manifested in his divine form. After severely chastising the demon, the Lord broke the demon's sword into two and then destroyed all his other weapons too. The battle between the two went on for quite some time. Realizing that Lord Shiva was deliberately exerting himself, Narad Muni requested the Lord, 'Dear Lord! Why are you using weapons against one who could be killed if you willed it? Please destroy him at once and do not play with him any longer.' Hearing the great sage's request, Lord Shiva simply made a devastating sound (*hunkar*) from his mouth, and the demon turned into ashes in an instant. The lord then destroyed his other associates as well.

Finally seeing an end to the prolonged misery brought about by the demon, everyone was delighted and wholeheartedly offered prayers of gratitude and glorification to the Lord.

However, saintly people are always concerned about others' welfare. They requested the Lord to continue to reside in that place to bless all who would visit in the future, and to purify it as it had been rendered impure by the sinful activities of the demon. Lord Shiva happily accepted and manifested as a jyotirlinga, which became famous as the Bhimashankar Jyotirlinga, for having killed the mighty demon Bhima.

The sages also declared, 'Anyone who sees you in this place would be immensely blessed, and this form of yours would relieve people of all miseries.'

Since then, the merciful Lord Shiva had been residing in this place, blessing countless souls who visit him year after year.

Location: Pune, on the Banks of River Bhima.

Timings: Every day from 4.30 a.m. to 12 noon and 4 p.m. to 9.30 p.m.

Nearest Railway Station: Karjat

7. Vishwanath

Vishwanath Jyotirlinga, the most revered and adored jyotirlinga, also known as Avi Mukteshwar Jyotirlinga, is situated in Kashi, the favourite city and capital of Lord Shiva.

Lord Shiva lived happily on the sacred Mount Kailash. He did not even have a house of his own, though he rewarded his worshippers with abundant material facilities. One day, Mother Parvati requested him to create a beautiful place where they could reside in seclusion. Understanding her desire, Lord Shiva created in the sky, a beautiful garden measuring five *kroshas* (15 km) known as 'Anandvan', meaning 'the place of happiness'. The location was extremely delightful for both the mind and other senses. Upon Lord Shiva's request, Lord Vishnu personally came to reside in this enchanting land and purify it further by His presence. As Lord Vishnu sat there in deep, intense meditation, He started sweating and as a result of his sweat, a huge water body was created around Anandvan. As the water levels rose, Anandvan came to be in danger of sinking. Sensing the imminent calamity, Lord Shiva lifted the entire land on His trident, thus preserving its true glory.

Mother Parvati, for whose pleasure this beautiful creation had been made, did not want to enjoy this land alone. Just like any mother who had selfless love for all her children in the material world and would always want them to share the same joy, she wanted everyone to experience the same bliss. Thus, she requested Lord Shiva to make some suitable arrangements. Understanding her loving affection for all her children, Lord Shiva placed this beautiful land from his trident onto the earth. This land, in due course, became famous as Kashi—the city of Light (enlightenment) and Varanasi—the land on the banks of two rivers 'Varuna' and 'Asi'. Then to always bless those who visit this sacred city in the future, Lord Shiva personally manifested here as a jyotirlinga, which became famous as Vishwanath (the lord of the world).

Shiva Purana explains that by simply having a darshan of the Vishwanath Jyotirlinga, we get the benefits of visiting all the other jyotirlingas as it is the most powerful one.

The temple housing this jyotirlinga is known as the Kashi Vishwanath Temple (see Chapter 13). A simple glimpse of the jyotirlinga is a soul-cleansing experience that transforms life and puts it on the path of knowledge and bhakti. Known as Vishweshwara Jyotirlinga, it has a very special and unique significance in the spiritual history of India.

Location: Varanasi on the banks of the Ganga

Timings: The temple generally opens around 3 a.m. with the mangala aarti and closes around 11 p.m. after the shringar aarti.

Timings may vary slightly on special occasions and festivals.

Nearest Railway Station: Varanasi Junction (often referred to as Varanasi Cantt)

8. Trimbakeshwar

Long ago, there lived a sage called Gautam, who was married to Ahalya, an extremely pious lady. He lived at Brahmagiri mountain (towards the south of India) and performed severe austerities for 10,000 years. Once, there was a severe drought in his area for 100 years, making everyone's life immensely difficult. Not a drop of water could be found anywhere. Everyone, including the sages, ordinary people, animals, birds and the beasts, left the place and went in different directions to find some hope.

The sage Gautam, in order to deal with this extreme situation, performed severe penances for six months to please Varuna, the celestial god in charge of water bodies. Being satisfied with the sage's endeavour, Varuna appeared and told him to ask for a boon. Gautam requested for the supply of water to resume in the area.

Delighted by his request, Varuna told sage Gautam, 'Since you have pleased me very much, I shall certainly fulfil your desire. Going against the regular protocol of the celestial gods, where they shower rain only at specific times and under certain conditions, I will arrange a source of water for you that will never diminish. Please dig a hole.'

As per Varuna's instruction, the sage quickly dug a hole equal in depth to one hand. Immediately, Varuna filled it up with celestial water that would never end. He further told the sage 'This water will become a holy tirtha and become famous by your name. Any charity, sacrifice, austerity or worship of the celestials and ancestors performed here will also bear eternal benefits.'

After saying this, Varuna disappeared, and sage Gautam, having become the instrument of compassion for others in the area by manifesting the much-needed water, felt completely satisfied.

This is the hallmark quality of a saintly person. A saintly person is not someone who wears saffron robes, has many followers, speaks very eloquently, lives in a monastery or knows scriptures by heart. The real saintly person is the one who is happy in others' happiness and is sad when others are sad. Sage Gautam was a real saint. No one had asked him to undergo difficult austerities, but he could not bear to see others suffering in the drought. He voluntarily took it upon himself to relieve everyone of this miserable situation. A saintly person does not mind going through pain in order to bring joy to others.

The world is sustained only on four principles: humility, compassion, selfless service and control of the senses. If these are gone, it becomes a difficult place to survive in.

Sage Gautam, feeling extremely satisfied and fortunate to have received the blessed and inexhaustible celestial waters, resumed his daily religious duties. He grew sufficient quantities of grains required for daily yajnas and in no time, the entire forest became beautified with a variety of flowers, fruit trees and plants. Thousands of birds, beasts, sages and other people flocked to the area to take advantage of the prosperity manifested due to sage Gautam's austerities.

The forest became the most charming spot on earth. Due to the presence of the blessed waters, no one suffered from the lack of seasonal rainfalls. Many saintly persons along with their disciples, wives and children, began to reside in the area and grew crops keeping in mind the future, if at all they were to face another drought. Due to sage Gautam's selfless service, the entire land became submerged in inexplicable bliss.

Once, the wives of certain brahmans who had come to reside near Sage Gautam's hermitage and were extremely proud of their high birth, took objection to Ahalya, Sage Gautam's wife, when she drew water from the same source. They considered Ahalya to be of low birth and therefore got upset at her for being around the same time as them to fetch water. Back at home, they instigated their husbands to harm Sage Gautam and his wife by performing a ritual to please Lord Ganesh. When Lord Ganesh appeared and asked them to ask for a boon, the ungrateful brahmans said, 'Dear Lord! If you are pleased with us then kindly help us make an arrangement that allows us to oust Gautam and his wife from this region.'

Lord Ganesh was surprised and advised them by saying:

Dear Sages! Listen carefully to what I am about to say. This will bring you good fortune. If you try to exhibit your anger towards Gautam and Ahalya, who have done nothing to harm you, it is not them who will get harmed. If someone has done some good to us and we, being ungrateful, try to cause them pain, all our good fortune will be finished in no time. To hurt someone who has shown us favour in the past is to follow the path of our destruction

All of you have performed great penance to please me and such endeavours should not be allowed to go to waste. You must use this opportunity to do good to yourselves and to others too. However, it seems what Lord Brahma has said is true. A saintly person never gives up his quality of saintliness and that is to show compassion to others, and an imposter can never be a saint. Earlier, when all of you were suffering, it was Sage Gautam's generosity that saved your lives. And now you want to trouble him? It is not at all advisable to tread this dangerous and impious path. Deliberate on it. Do not act as henpecked husbands. If you do not act as per my advice, forget harming Gautam, on the contrary, your actions will end up doing more good to him. Even if you try to hurt him, he will still continue to be your well-wisher since he is a true saint. Therefore, do not do this. Ask for another benediction.

Lord Ganesh is everyone's well-wisher, and thus he tried to impart some wisdom to the immature sages. But unfortunately, his words fell on deaf ears and the brahmans continued to be insistent. Lord Ganesh was duty-bound to give a boon to anyone who performed austerities to petition him, and so he granted their request with a final warning to be ready for the consequences of their plans. After that, he quietly left for his abode.

One day, Lord Ganesh took the form of an emaciated cow, entered the fields of Sage Gautam and started eating the crop. When the sage saw her, he came running and to save the grains, picked a few, delicate blades of grass and gently touched them to the cow in an attempt to move her out of the field. However, as soon as he did it, the cow instantly fell dead. The envious brahmans, along with their wives and disciples, were watching this unfold secretly and took this as an opportunity to pounce upon this golden opportunity. They then came out of their hiding and started ridiculing Sage Gautam for having killed a cow. The virtuous sage was heartbroken. He called his wife and expressed his sorrow thus: 'What has just happened? It looks like the Supreme Lord is displeased with me. What should I do now? Where do I go? I have killed a cow, the symbol of dharma.'

The ungrateful brahmans, along with their families and followers, continued to shout at Gautam and Ahalya. 'Get out of here. We cannot see your face. You are a cow killer. If anyone even sees the face of such a person, he must immediately jump into a river with clothes on to purify himself. You do not deserve to live here. Leave this place at once.'

They also threw stones at the couple and verbally abused them. Being threatened and insulted, the humble sage agreed to leave the place and go elsewhere with his wife. The duo came to a relatively distant spot in the forest and settled there. But even there, they were not allowed to live in peace. The envious brahmans came and barred the sage from performing any Vedic rituals as he was, according to them, a sinner and thus unqualified to do so. Sage Gautam spent some time bereft of his religious duties but when he could not bear it any longer, he humbly requested them to tell him the way to purify himself.

The proud brahmans said, 'To get rid of your sin, you must circumambulate the earth thrice, and then come here and completely fast for one month. Then circumambulate the Brahmagiri mountain 100 times. After this, you will be freed from your sin. Another way to do this would be that you bring the sacred Ganga here and after bathing in her waters, make 10 million shivalings and worship Lord Shiva. Then bathe in the Ganga and circumambulate the Brahmagiri mountain eleven times. Follow it up with the bathing of the shivaling with water from 100 pots. This way, you will get thoroughly purified of your sinful act.'

Sage Gautam humbly accepted and did as the brahmans instructed. He made shivalings out of mud and worshipped them devoutly with his blessed wife. During this period of worship and austerities, they were duly served and taken care of by their disciples.

Being immensely satisfied with their sincere worship, one fine day, Lord Shiva appeared before them with his associates and spoke, 'I am extremely pleased with your mode of worship. Please ask for whatever you desire.'

Sage Gautam was overwhelmed with ecstasy upon seeing the Lord and fell at his feet. After offering prayers of glorification and gratitude to the Lord, he requested the Lord for the boon of becoming free from the sin that he had inadvertently committed.

The kind Lord informed the sage that he had always been sinless and that the brahmans had cheated him. Lord Shiva glorified him by saying, 'You are so pure that just by seeing you, everyone becomes free from sins. So how could you be sinful? Those who have tried to harm you are the most sinful. They are ungrateful and will never be delivered from their sinful reactions. They all are doomed. They are so impure that if anyone happens to see them, that person will become inflicted with sins.'

Sage Gautam, who never saw anyone's faults, was astonished to hear this and thus spoke, 'My dear Lord! Those brahmans have actually done me the greatest favour by behaving the way they did. If they did not act the way they had, how would I have gotten your audience? Thus, those brahmans are actually my well-wishers.'

Lord Shiva was delighted to hear the sage's words, which were so full of humility and wisdom. Thus he spoke, 'Dear Gautam! You are the best. You are the greatest of saintly personalities. Please ask for any boon.'

Gautam replied, 'Dear Lord! If you are really pleased with me, then bless me with the presence of the sacred

Ganga here.' Saying this, he held the feet of Lord Shiva with great yearning.

On the desire of Lord Shiva, Ganga appeared in her personified form. Sage Gautam humbly bowed down to her and requested her to purify him. Lord Shiva instructed her to do the same and stay on earth till the twenty-eighth Kaliyuga of Vaivasvat Manu.[61] The present period is that period. This means that the Ganga will soon disappear from this planet.

Goddess Ganga requested, 'If my glory will supersede that of other rivers and if you also agree to stay here with Goddess Ambika (another name for Mother Parvati, Lord Shiva's wife), I will be elated.' Lord Shiva happily consented to her request. As Ganga glorified and thanked Lord Shiva for his kindness, the celestial gods, sages and holy places in their personified forms appeared there and offered their respects.

Being pleased, Lord Shiva and Ganga offered them a boon. The celestial gods requested, 'We would be so grateful if both of you could bless us and other beings by staying here.'

Upon hearing their request, Mother Ganga replied that she had especially come for Sage Gautam's benefit. She had planned to return as she had come, but she was happy to stay at the place provided by the celestials because it proved her special stature in their society.

In order to assure her of their special respect for her, the celestial gods and sages replied, 'Whenever the planet Jupiter appears in the Leo zodiac, we will come here to reside.

---

[61] The Manu ruling the present millennium.

We shall come to you to purify ourselves by bathing in your waters and taking the darshan of Lord Shiva. Only after getting your permission, we shall leave from here and return to our respective abodes after Jupiter moves out of Leo. Thus, please stay here with Lord Shiva to bless us.'

Upon their request, Lord Shiva and Mother Ganga established themselves in the place. The Ganga became famous as Gautami Ganga and the manifested jyotirlinga became the celebrated Trimbakeshwar.

Since that day, whenever Jupiter is in Leo, all the celestial gods leave their heavenly abodes and reside on the banks of Gautami Ganga.

Location: Foothills of the Brahmagiri mountains in Nasik, Maharashtra

Timings: 5.30 a.m. to 9 p.m., all days of the week.

How to Reach: The nearest airport to Trimbakeshwar is the Chhatrapati Shivaji International Airport, Mumbai. The nearest railway station is Igatpuri.

Located in Nashik, Trimbakeshwar can be reached by road too.

9. Baidyanath

The mighty demon Ravana, extremely proud of his strength, was busy performing severe austerities to please Lord Shiva at Mount Kailash. Unable to get the audience of the most compassionate Lord Shiva, Ravana decided to intensify and change the course of his efforts. He dug a hole in the ground in the forest south of the Himalayas and lit a sacrificial fire in it. Right next to the fire, he also made and installed a shivaling for worship.

During the summer, he would sit in the middle surrounded by fire on all sides. He would lay in the open ground during the torrential monsoons and stand in cold waters during the winter season. He continued such austerities for a long time but still, the object of his worship was nowhere to be seen. Desperate, he took to an extremely ghastly practice.

Famous as Dashashan—the one with ten heads—Ravana, in order to force Lord Shiva to appear before him, began cutting off his heads and offering them into the fire one after the other. Even after sacrificing nine of his ten heads, when the most merciful Lord Shiva did not appear, he started preparing to cut off his last head. Just as he was about to do so, Lord Shiva, taking mercy on him and feeling pity, manifested in front of the demon in his majestic form. He reinstated all the heads of the demon to their original position and blessed Ravana with immense strength as per his desire.

Delighted at having gotten what he wanted, the demon prayed, 'Dear Lord! Be pleased with me. I want to take you to Lanka. Please fulfil this desire of mine. I have come to seek your shelter.'

Lord Shiva was perplexed. 'Why would I go to live in a demon's kingdom?' he thought. He told Ravana to instead take the shivaling to Lanka as he (Lord Shiva) resided in it. But there was a condition. Lord Shiva told him not to put the shivaling anywhere on the ground before he reached Lanka. Once having touched the ground, the shivaling would not budge from that place. Ravana happily accepted the arrangement.

He picked up the shivaling and began travelling home across the ocean in the south. But on the way, due to Lord Shiva's inspiration, the demon developed the urge to respond to nature's call. Unable to control it, he looked around and saw a cowherd boy standing close by. After putting the shivaling in his hands and requesting him to carefully hold it, he ran into the forest. Since he did not return for a relatively long time, the cowherd boy got tired of holding the shivaling and put it down on the ground before going home. When Ravana eventually returned and tried to lift the shivaling, it would not move. Accepting the inevitable and feeling happy at having received tremendous powers from Lord Shiva, he returned to Lanka and narrated the events to his wife Mandodari. This sacred shivaling became famous in the world by the name of Baidyanath Jyotirlinga.

After the news of Ravana having received powers from Lord Shiva reached the celestial gods, they became increasingly worried and requested Narada Muni, the foremost of the sages, to think of a remedy. Narada, who is the well-wisher of everyone, went to Ravana and instigated him to test his newly acquired strength by trying to lift the mighty Mount Kailash. This would verify whether Lord Shiva's boon worked. Ravana liked the idea and sped towards Kailash. Using his immense power, he uprooted Kailash, as a result of which the entire mountain shook. This sudden movement greatly disturbed Mother Parvati, who requested Lord Shiva to teach the perpetrator a lesson. Lord Shiva angrily cursed Ravana, 'You rascal! You are so proud of your strength? You just wait. The personality who will humble you and smash your pride will soon be born.'

Ravana, seemingly undeterred by the curse and feeling a sense of accomplishment having successfully tested his strength, proudly returned to Lanka.

Meanwhile, when the celestial gods and sages heard the news of the manifestation of the jyotirlinga, they eagerly came to behold the beautiful darshan of the Lord and performed its installation according to the proper Vedic procedure. After having duly worshipped it to their heart's content and giving it the name Baidyanath, they returned to the heavens.

Location: Deoghar in Jharkhand.

Timings: Open on all seven days from 4 a.m. to 3.30 p.m. and from 6 p.m. to 9 p.m.

During special religious occasions like Mahashivaratri, darshan timings are stretched.

How to Reach: The nearest railway station is Jasidih Junction. This station can be reached from Ranchi. The temple is just 15 km away from the station and can be reached in an auto or a cab.

10. Nageshwar

Upon receiving special boons from Goddess Parvati (wife of Lord Shiva), Daruka, a mighty demoness, had grown excessively proud. Along with their demon associates, Daruka and her husband, Daruk, wreaked havoc everywhere by killing saintly people, and destroying all yajnas and other acts of religion.

Along the shore of the ocean towards the western side of India, there was a beautiful forest replete with all types of prosperity. It spread over an area of sixteen yojanas (one yojana is 8 miles). The forest belonged to Goddess Parvati, but she had made Daruka its caretaker. The forest had a mystical ability—wherever Daruka went, the entire forest would also go with her. She would sport in that forest with her husband to her heart's content. However, their presence in the forest and the violence they created was a source of great anxiety for the other beings living there. As a result, one fine day, all the residents of the forest went to sage Aurav for help and desperately narrated their ordeal. Considering it his duty to give protection to those who sought his shelter, sage Aurav pronounced a curse, 'If at all these demons commit any further acts of violence towards anyone, they would immediately die.'

When the celestial gods heard the news, they saw an opportunity in this extraordinary turn of events and immediately attacked the demons. The demons were caught in a very bewildering situation. If they retaliated in any way, they would fall dead. And if they did not, they would be defeated and killed anyway.

Fearing for their lives, Daruka moved the entire forest along with her demon associates into the ocean and began to reside underwater without any fear. However, their presence and demonic acts began to create great anxiety for the aquatics now.

One day, a fleet of boats filled with human beings happened to come there. As soon as they arrived in the area, the demons arrested everyone, put them inside the prison and threatened them in innumerable ways. The leader of the fleet was a merchant named Supriya, who was gentle, pious and a great devotee of Lord Shiva. He always wore rudraksha beads and smeared ashes on his body, symbolic of his immense faith in and allegiance to Lord Shiva.

He would not eat until he had finished his daily worship of Lord Shiva and had even trained his friends in the proper procedure of worshipping his deity. Inspired by his example, everyone in the fleet had become a sincere follower of Lord Shiva. So when they were caught, they naturally began to call out to their Lord for help. When the news reached the demons, they threatened Supriya and ran after him to kill him. Seeing them approaching with evil intentions, Supriya was filled with fear and began to remember Lord Shiva. He chanted his names and prayed with great love, 'O most merciful Lord! Please save me. You are everything to me and I am yours. You are my life and soul and I take complete shelter in you. Please protect me.'

Moved by the prayers of his dear devotee, Lord Shiva appeared on the scene along with a magnificent temple that had four gates. In the middle of that gorgeous structure lay the most radiant jyotirlinga and seated next to it was the entire family of Lord Shiva. Supriya worshipped the jyotirlinga in great ecstasy. Pleased by his worship, Lord Shiva took up his ultimate weapon, the Pashupatastra, and personally destroyed the prominent demons along with their weapons and associates. Thereafter, in order to make the forest a safe place to reside in, the Lord blessed the forest and safe, 'From today, may all the four social orders of society—Brahmins, Kshatriyas, Vaishyas and Shudras stay peacefully in this forest. May all the saintly people make it their home and may it remain forbidden for demons forever.'

When she heard this unique arrangement of Lord Shiva, the worried Daruka invoked the mercy of her deity,

Goddess Parvati. When Mother Parvati appeared and asked Daruka to request a boon, Daruka fervently prayed to her to protect her dynasty. Promising to do so, Mother Parvati, who is the mother of material beings and thus most kind-hearted, turned to Lord Shiva and spoke thus, 'Dear Lord! May this proclamation become true at the end of Kaliyuga. Till then, please allow the demonic beings to stay and flourish. I also belong to you and therefore, please fulfil my desire as you have fulfilled Supriya's. This demoness Daruka is my shakti only. She is the most powerful. Please bless that she rules the demon's kingdom and whenever the demonesses give birth to any children, may they be allowed to live in this forest. This is my desire.'

Lord Shiva, who is compassion personified, happily consented and declared thus, 'I will stay in this forest to nourish the devotees and whoever will take my darshan here will become the conqueror of the world. At the end of Kaliyuga and the beginning of Satyayuga, Virasena, the son of King Mahasena, will be the king of all kings. He will be my great devotee and a great warrior. He will come here and after seeing me, will be crowned as the conqueror of the world in no time.'

After showering nectar into the ears of their worshippers through their sweet conversations, Lord Shiva and Mother Parvati happily began to reside in that area. Lord Shiva became famous as Nageshwar and Mother Parvati began to be glorified by the name Nageshwari. Anyone who hears or studies this narration of the manifestation of the Nageshwar Jyotirlinga will become free from all sinful karmas.

Location: Near Dwarka, Gujarat

Timings: The temple usually opens at 6 a.m. and closes by 9 p.m. However, it's always a good idea to confirm the timings by checking the temple's official website or contacting local authorities, especially during festivals or special events.

How to Reach: The nearest railway station is Dwarka, located 17 km from the temple. Upon arrival at the station, one can hire taxis and rickshaws or avail of local transportation services to reach Nageshwar Jyotirlinga. Nageshwar is well-connected by road—state-run buses and private bus services ply regularly between major cities of Gujarat and Nageshwar.

11. Rameshwar

The Supreme Lord, in order to re-establish and protect religious principles, and set the highest standards of morality and conduct for all human beings, appeared as Lord Ramchandra in the Tretayuga. When He performed the pastime of being exiled to the forest for fourteen years, His beloved wife Sita (an incarnation of Goddess Laxmi) was abducted by a demon named Ravana. To bring her back, He became friends with Sugriva, the king of the *vanaras* (monkeys), who sent four teams in four different directions to look for Mother Sita. The team with Hanuman was successful in collecting information about her whereabouts and related how she was confined inside Ashok Vatika, the royal gardens of Ravana in Lanka, across the ocean. Eventually, everyone gathered at the ocean to march towards Ravana's kingdom, but a great obstacle lay in between—the mighty ocean. Everyone was anxious. At that time, Lord Ram decided to pray to Lord

Shiva for help. Lord Shiva is Bhubhneswar, the master of the material world, and Lord Ram is the ideal human being. Here, he showed by example how Lord Shiva is to be respected. Even within the universe, whenever there is trouble, the presiding deities of the universe can approach Lord Brahma for help and if he cannot resolve the issue, he takes everyone to Lord Shiva. And if Lord Shiva also cannot help, they all go to Lord Vishnu, who lies on the bed of Ananta-shesha (the divine serpent), in an ocean of milk called Kshira-sagar. So it is not improper for Lord Ram to worship Lord Shiva.

Furthermore, Ravana was a devotee of Lord Shiva, and Lord Ram did not want to kill him unless it was sanctioned by Lord Shiva himself. Therefore, he wanted to inform Lord Shiva about his mission by enacting the pastime of seeking his blessings in person. He wanted to convey, 'Look! I am going to kill your devotee. Hope you do not mind.' And this plan would be authorized if Lord Shiva announced his blessings for Lord Ram's victory.

Thus, Lord Ram made a shivaling out of mud and began worshipping it with utmost love and devotion according to the proper Vedic procedure. Being called for with such feeling, Lord Shiva manifested there in his effulgent form along with Mother Parvati on his left side and other devout associates. Lord Ram asked for blessings to be victorious in battle against the king of Lanka and Lord Shiva, understanding the pastime of the Lord, happily said, 'So be it!'

Lord Ram also requested Lord Shiva to reside at the place eternally to bless all its visitors in the future. Lord Shiva consented and this, in turn, came to be known as Rameshwaram Jyotirlinga, which means *ram yasya ishvaram*—the one (Lord Shiva) whose Lord is Ram. Rameshwaram also happens to be one of the four main dhams of Lord Vishnu (Badrinath in the North, Jagannath Puri in the East, Dwarka in the West and Rameshwaram in the south).

Location: Rameswaram, Tamil Nadu

Timings: Opens at 5 a.m. with the morning rituals and closes by 9 p.m. after the evening ceremonies. As timings can shift during festivals and special occasions, it's recommended to check the temple's official website or consult with local temple authorities for the most current timings.

How to Reach: Rameswaram has its own railway station, which is well-connected to several major cities across India. The station is close to the temple, making it convenient for travellers. Rameswaram is also accessible by road from various parts of Tamil Nadu and neighbouring states. State-run buses as well as private bus services operate regularly to and from Rameswaram.

12. Grishneshwar

(Also known as Ghushmeshwar and Kusumeshwar)

Near the beautiful Devagiri mountain in the South, there once resided a brahman named Sudharma, who belonged to the illustrious family lineage of the great sage Bharadvaj. Sudharma's chaste wife, Sudeha, an expert in household duties, was always absorbed in devotion to Lord Shiva and serving her husband.

Sudharma was respectful towards everyone, especially the celestial gods and the guests. He would regularly perform his religious duties and follow the path of righteousness. Well-versed in the Vedic scriptures, he taught the same to his disciples. He was wealthy and at the same time charitable. Not only was he himself a great devotee of Lord Shiva, but he had great affection for all other devotees as well.

But we live in a world in which no one is spared. Even if there are a thousand things going our way, there will be at least one thing that makes our life miserable. Despite all their piety and goodwill, the brahman couple was not happy since they did not have a child. While Sudharma accepted this, Sudeha was unable to come to terms with this. Sudharma would often counsel her, but she would not listen. Finally, just to experience the happiness of a child within the house, Sudeha decided to get Sudharma married to her sister, Ghushma. Sudharma tried to caution her that this was not the best thing to do and that it would cause conflict among the sisters, but Sudeha was confident that no such thing would happen.

After marriage, Ghushma came into the house and humbly, like a maidservant, started serving her elder sister. Sudeha also showered immense affection upon Ghushma and the duo seemed inseparable. As per the guidance and instructions of her elder sister, Ghushma would make 100 shivalings daily and duly worship them before immersing them in the pond nearby.

By the blessings of Lord Shiva, Ghushma, in due course, gave birth to a wonderful son who seemed to possess all divine qualities. As a result, Ghushma's fame increased, and this triggered envy in Sudeha's heart. When the boy got married and his wife came into the house, Sudeha's envy increased a million-fold. Unable to bear it any longer, one night, Sudeha killed Ghushma's son as he was resting and chopped his body into small pieces, which she then threw into the same pond where Ghushma would immerse her shivalings. After accomplishing her mission, Sudeha came back home and happily slept. After all, the biggest obstacle in her life was finally gone.

Meanwhile, Ghushma and Sudharma woke up in the morning and busied themselves with their morning duties. Sudeha got up and engaged herself in household chores too. She was much happier on this day, though she did not express it. When the daughter-in-law woke up, to her horror, she found the bed covered in blood and a few pieces of her husband's body. She ran to Sudharma and Ghushma, informing them about the ghastly incident. Sudeha superficially cried while hiding her inner bliss. But Ghushma, despite hearing the terrible news, did not leave her worship of Lord Shiva and continued undisturbed. Sudharma was no different. Not leaving their worship midway was indicative of their dedication to their deity.

It was after almost half a day that Ghushma went to see her son's bed where the heinous act had taken place. She remained unaffected. Remembering Lord Shiva, she thought, 'The one who gave me the son will also protect him. He is the well-wisher of his devotees. He is Mahakal (death personified) and the shelter of the saintly people. He is our only shelter. What will I gain by being anxious?' Thus, she refused to lament. As per her daily routine, she picked up all the shivalings and carried them to the pond for immersion. As she turned around after immersing them, she found her son standing on the banks, with a blissful smile.

Even after seeing her son alive, Ghushma remained equiposed. She was not sad when she had lost him and now, when he came back, she was not elated. Immensely pleased with her disposition, Lord Shiva appeared on the scene and told her, 'Please ask for a boon. Your cunning sister had killed your son. I will destroy her with my trident.'

However, Ghushma, being a gentle, pious soul, disagreed with Lord Shiva. She replied, 'My dear Lord! Sudeha is my sister. You should protect her.'

When the Lord insisted that Sudeha deserved to be killed, Ghushma humbly said, 'Dear Lord! May her sins be destroyed when she sees you. The one who offers kindness to those who wrong him gains the strength to erase the misdeeds of those who merely look at him. She might have done something wrong, but why should I give up my nature?'

Lord Shiva became even more ecstatic hearing these nectarine words. He requested Ghushma to ask for another boon as he wanted to bless her profusely.

On being asked by the Lord, Ghushma requested, 'My Lord! If you wish to offer a benediction, please stay here forever to protect everyone.'

Lord Shiva happily agreed and declared that he would reside at the place as a jyotirlinga, known as Ghusmesh Jyotirlinga—the Lord of Ghushma. And the pond will become the residence of many shivalings and turn famous by the name 'Shivalaya'.

The Lord further blessed Ghushma, 'Your next 100 generations will be blessed with equally powerful and virtuous sons, who are equipped with all facilities for material enjoyment as well as divine qualities. They will be clever, knowledgeable and have a long lifespan. Your entire lineage will remain glorious for a hundred generations to come.'

Saying this, Lord Shiva turned into a jyotirlinga, which became glorified as Gushmeshwar or Grishneshwar.

Right after Sudharma, Sudeha and Ghushma circumambulated the jyotirlinga 100 times. Sudeha felt embarrassed seeing Ghushma's son and begged for forgiveness. She sincerely engaged herself in atonement for her sin, and forgetting all the unpleasant episodes that had taken place, they all lived happily ever after.

Location: Near Aurangabad in Maharashtra

Timings: The temple usually opens around 5.30 a.m. and closes by 9.30 p.m. However, timings might differ on special occasions and festivals.

How to Reach: The nearest railway station is Chhatrapati Sambhajinagar (previously known as Aurangabad). Taxis, auto-rickshaws and buses operate from the station to the temple. Ghrishneshwar is well-connected by road. Regular state transport buses and private buses ply between Chhatrapati Sambhajinagar and the temple. Given its proximity to the Ellora Caves, many tourists opt to visit both destinations in a single trip.

Chapter 17

Lord Shiva in Vrindavan

Lord Shiva is also known as Lokpal or Dikpal as he protects the sacred places of Lord Krishna's pastimes.

Wherever there is a prominent Lord Krishna temple, a Shiva temple will be close by. In Vraja, also known as Vrindavan, he has manifested in various places to assist Lord Krishna in His pastimes and to help His devotees attain spiritual perfection.

The four ancient deities of Lord Shiva residing in the Mathura district are known as dikpals, 'protectors of the directions'. They stay in Mathura to protect the holy dham of Lord Krishna.

1. Bhuteshvara Mahadeva

Bhuteshvara Mahadeva protects the western side of Mathura.

The tradition among the devotees is that when coming to Braj, one must first go to Mathura to take permission from him to enter the dham. The reasons for this are described by Srila Rupa Gosvami, a great Vaishnav acharya from Vrindavan, in his Mathura-Mahatmya (texts 234–38). He quotes the following verses from the Adi-Varaha Purana, recounting Lord Krishna's words about Bhuteshvara Mahadeva:

> O deva! You will be the protector of Mathura. O greatest of the gods! Whoever sees you will attain My abode. By seeing Bhuteshvara Mahadeva, all sins are destroyed. O Vasudha (Goddess Bhumi)! The one who sees him achieves the land of Mathura. In Mathura is the deity of Lord Bhuteshvara, who grants liberation even to the sinful. This deity is very dear to Me. How can a sinful person who worships Me, but fails to worship Bhuteshvara Shiva, ever attain devotion to Me? Those who are bewildered by My maya, who are the lowest of men, will not meditate on, bow down before or offer prayers to Lord Bhuteshvara.

Also, the famous scripture Chaitanya Charitamrta (Madhya 17.191) by Krishnadasa Kaviraja Gosvami describes how Lord Chaitanya, the combined avatar of Radha–Krishna in one form, visited Bhuteshvara Mahadeva in the following way:

'Shri Chaitanya Mahaprabhu visited all the holy places on the banks of the Yamuna, including Svayambhu, Vishrama Ghat, Dirgha Lord Vishnu, Bhuteshvara Mahadeva and Gokarna.'

2. Gopishvar Mahadeva

Gopishvar Mahadeva is one of the most prominent deities among devotees and is mentioned in many Vaishnav works of literature, being a very ancient protector of Shri Vrindavan Dham. One cannot enter Vrindavan without his permission. His glories are sung throughout Vaishnav literature:

'I offer my respectful obeisances to Shri Gopishvar, who is merciful Lord Shiva himself. He removes troubles and grants spiritual love in Vrindavan.' (Bhakti Ratnakar 5.3741)

In the famous song 'Vraja-dhama-mahimamrta' written by the great Vaishnav poet Krishna Das, the following line is sung:

'Jaya jaya gopishwara Vrindavan majha'

'All glories, all glories to Gopishvara Shiva, who resides in the holy dham of Vrindavan.'

The following episode gives the account of how Lord Shiva manifested as Gopishvar Mahadeva:

Once while in deep meditation on Mount Kailash, Lord Shiva heard the sweet vibration of Lord Krishna playing His divine flute. Mesmerized, he entered samadhi. He followed that transcendental sound until he came to Vrindavan, where Lord Gopinath was getting ready to start the *maharaas*[62] with His gopis.

Desiring intensely to join the maharaas, when he came to the entrance of the arena of the raas-dance, he was stopped by Paurnamasi,[63] who told him, 'No males except

---

[62] Lord Krishna's divine dance.

[63] An incarnation of Yogamaya (Krishna's energy).

Lord Krishna are allowed entry here. First, you must have a *gopi-rupa*, the form of a Vraja milkmaid, a gopi. Only then can you enter.'

Lord Bholanath asked, 'How can I get gopi-rupa?' Yogamaya replied, 'Seek the shelter of Vrinda Devi. She will grant you the form of a gopi.'

Vrinda Devi asked Lord Shiva to take a dip in the waters of Manasarovar. After bathing there, Lord Shiva emerged from the lake in the form of a beautiful gopi.

Vrinda Devi then took Lord Shiva, in her gopi form, to one corner of the raas-sthali. Lord Shiva stood there and prayed to Sri Sri Radha Krishna to attain pure devotion to Them.

Then the raas started. Lord Krishna danced with all the gopis. He also danced elegantly with Lord Shiva disguised as a gopi.

Then, after some time, when they were resting, the Lord said, 'I'm not getting the usual pleasure from our raas. Something is not right. I think there is another man in our midst.' He then asked Lalita Devi to check all the gopis and make sure no man was lurking around dressed as one of them.

Lalita Devi went around and lifted the veils of all the hundreds of gopis, but she couldn't find any man. She returned and reported to Lord Krishna, 'I have not found any man, but there is one gopi with three eyes.'

Lord Krishna asked her to bring her to Him. When the Lord saw the Shiva gopi, He laughed heartily and addressed him, 'O Gopishvar, I am very pleased to see you in the form of a gopi. But you know that this raas dance is not for householders. Therefore, since you have already participated and fulfilled your desire, I offer you the post of *raas-dwar paal*.[64] I also give you the blessing that henceforth, all the gopis will offer respect to you and seek your blessing to get gopi bhava.'

Since then, Gopishvar Mahadeva has been worshipped in Vrindavan in the form of a Shiva linga in the mornings. In the evenings, the shiva-linga is dressed up beautifully as a gopi and devotees pray to the same to be allowed to enter the raas lila, the highest pastime of love of Lord Krishna.

3. Kameshvara Mahadeva

Kama means 'desire'. Kameshvara Mahadeva, residing in the Kamyavan forest of Braj, is the fulfiller of one's desires.

Srila Narahari Chakravarti, a famous Vaishnav acharya, has described Kameshvara Mahadeva in his book Bhakti-Ratnakara (5.841):

'See here the most powerful Lord Shiva as
Kameshvara.'

According to the tradition in Vraja, Vrishabhanu Maharaj, the father of Radha, worshipped Kameshvara to get a daughter (he already had a son, Shridama, but also wanted a daughter). When Kameshvara granted his desire, he obtained the most glorious Srimati Radharani as his daughter.

---

[64] Gatekeeper of the raas dance.

4. Chakaleshvar Mahadeva

On the northern bank of Manasi Ganga, a beautiful lake by the sacred Govardhana hill, is a group of five shivalings that are known as Chakaleshvara Mahadeva. These five shivalings are considered to be Lord Shiva's five faces, which protect the area of Govardhan. This part of Manasi Ganga is known as Chakratirtha and because he stays at this place, this shivaling was originally known as Chakareshvara (now Chakaleshvara). It is said that this place is called Chakratirtha because when Lord Krishna lifted Govardhana Hill, He requested the Sudarshana Chakra to appear above the mountain to dry up all the rain coming down on Govardhana so that the *Vrajavasis*[65] standing underneath would not drown. After Indra withdrew the *samvartaka* clouds[66] that he had sent to destroy Vraja and the danger was over, Sudarshana requested Lord Krishna to give him a place to rest near Govardhan. Lord Krishna gave him this place on the northern bank of Manasi Ganga.

5. Nandishvar Mahadeva

The palace of Nanda Maharaja, Lord Krishna's father, is situated atop Nandishvar Hill in Nandgaon. This hill is a form of Lord Shiva, who performed austerities for several thousands of years to enter into Lord Krishna's pastimes in Vraja. When the Lord was pleased with him, Lord Shiva asked for the boon of obtaining a chance to witness the Vraja pastimes of Lord Krishna by becoming a hill or a

---

[65] Residents of Vraja.

[66] The clouds of devastation.

stone. In accordance with his desire, Lord Krishna granted him this form in Nandgaon.

Srila Visvanatha Chakravarti Thakura writes in Vraja-Riti-Chintamani (1.15):

> 'The devotees declare that Nandishvar Hill, the
>   form of Lord Shiva now shining as
> Nanda Maharaja's capital, is an endlessly
>   beautiful crown decorating Vrindavana.'

Lord Shiva has stayed at Nandgaon in the form of Nandishvar Mahadeva and even today, the *charanamrita*[67] and *mahaprasada*[68] of Lord Krishna are first offered to him.

Here is how Lord Shiva came to permanently reside at Nandgaon:

While Lord Shiva was in meditation, he discovered that Lord Krishna had been born in Vraja at the house of Nanda Maharaj.

On the twelfth day, after the birth of the Lord, Lord Shiva decided to go and visit Him at Gokul.

Lord Krishna was acting like a baby, performing His pastimes in the lap of Mother Yashoda.

Knowing that Nanda Maharaj generously gave charity to please the brahmanas, Lord Shiva decided to disguise himself as a brahmana and proceeded to Gokul to see Lord Krishna.

But as soon as he touched the dust of Vraja, he realized that he should not change his form.

---

[67] The sacred bathing water of Lord Krishna.

[68] Remnants of the food eaten by Lord Krishna first.

He thought, 'The Lord knows who I am, therefore I must go in my real form.'

Now, Lord Shiva's natural form has three eyes and long, matted hair. He wears tiger skin, a garland of snakes and a belt of scorpions, and has ashes smeared all over his body.

Exhibiting this fearsome form, he entered Gokul, proceeded to Mother Yashoda's house, and knocked on the door. He said, '*bhikhsham de hi* [give me alms].'

Mother Yashoda answered the door, but, in her deep, ecstatic love for Lord Krishna, did not recognize the visitor as Lord Shiva.

Yashoda, always generous to visiting saints, said, 'Wait outside. I will bring you a gift.'

Lord Shiva replied, 'No, no, I do not want any gifts. I have come here to see your son.'

Upon hearing the visitor's request, Mother Yashoda replied, 'No, it is not possible for you to see Him. Anything else you wish, you may have. I see you are hungry and in need of clothing. Please wait a moment, and I shall bring you some nice food and clean garments. Please take them and leave.'

Lord Shiva humbly replied, 'No, no, I have everything. My wife is Annapurna (another name for Parvati), whom I have left behind to come and see your son. Please allow me to see your son, even if only for a second.'

Hearing Lord Shiva's plea, Mother Yashoda firmly replied, 'Take what I give you and go before your snakes and scorpions fall here. Please understand that my baby is very small and will be frightened seeing your shabby appearance. So, please go.'

Knowing how determined Yashoda was, Lord Shiva said, 'I shall not go until I see your son.'

Mother Yashoda stood firm and said, 'You can sit here as long as you want, but you will not see my son.'

At this, Lord Shiva became desperate and expressed his resolve: 'I can sit here for 10,000 years. One day, when your son grows up and is no longer under your control, I will see Him then.'

Mother Yashoda was not to be moved. She said, 'O Babaji [respected saint], if you sit here for 10,000 years, I shall close this gate for 20,000 years. I will open a different gate through which my son will go out to play. Do not challenge me. My lovely son is my life.'

Meanwhile, Lord Krishna, lying on the bed, became aware of what was going on outside the door.

Lord Shiva acts as the ultimate devotee in a servitor role, while Mother Yashoda embodies pure devotion through the stronger and more powerful emotion of parental love. Both have unalloyed love for Lord Krishna, but in this case, parental love exists on a higher plane as compared to that of a servitor.

Lord Shiva was defeated and had to yield to Mother Yashoda in this confrontation.

Upon being defeated, Lord Shiva thought, 'O Krishna! You are the Lord of the universe hiding in the house of this cowherd lady. This is Your will, and if Your will is not to see me, what can I do?'

Thinking this, he said to Mother Yashoda, 'O lady, I am leaving but you will soon call me to see your son.'

Hearing this, Mother Yashoda replied, 'You go. I will not call you. You can take whatever else you wish, but do not ask me again to see my child.'

Lord Shiva left, feeling very morose. He reached the bank of the Yamuna River, sat down and began meditating on how dramatically Lord Krishna acts.

Lord Krishna, knowing that His best devotee left the house disappointed, began to cry, and no one could stop Him.

All the *gopas*[69] and gopis tried to console Him but all attempts failed. He continued crying loudly.

A clever gopi named Lalita approached Mother Yashoda and asked her if anyone had left the house dissatisfied.

Mother Yashoda thought for a moment and said, 'Yes, one mendicant came with snakes wrapped around his neck and wanted to see my child. I wanted to give him whatever he desired, but he insisted that he only wished to see Him. He did not take anything and left, looking sad.'

Lalita then said, 'A saintly person should never leave one's house dissatisfied. Whatever he wanted, he should have been given. This is the curse that is haunting your baby and all of us. Therefore, we must call him back.'

Mother Yashoda, being the greatest well-wisher of her child and willing to do anything to please Him, described the appearance of the visitor and sent some people to look for him. They soon found him and brought him back to the house.

Mother Yashoda handed the crying baby Lord Krishna to Lord Shiva.

As soon as Lord Krishna was in Lord Shiva's arms, He immediately stopped crying, opened His eyes and saw His beloved associate.

---

[69] Cowherd boys.

Lord Shiva, finally holding the object of his love to his chest, was lost in ecstasy.

He prayed, 'O Lord of the universe, O Lord of all, O supreme controller, it is very difficult to ascertain how You will act next. It is inconceivable that the Lord who cannot be seen by meditating for thousands of years, is now acting as the child of a cowherd lady! Only You know Your desire. No one else does. O Lord, I simply pay my homage unto You.'

After saying this, Lord Shiva took the Lord's little feet, touched them to his head and chanted the 'Gopala Sahasranam Stotra [1000 names of the Gopal (Krishna)].' He later repeated these names to Parvati when he returned home.

Upon seeing this, Mother Yashoda said, 'Baba, watch your snakes. My child is very small.'

Hearing this, Lord Shiva realized the superiority of the devotion of Mother Yashoda and understood why Lord Krishna had appeared as her son.

Seeing how Lord Krishna had stopped crying instantly after seeing him, she requested Lord Shiva to stay at her home so that whenever Lord Krishna would cry, she would bring Him to see him and the baby would immediately get pacified. Lord Shiva happily accepted the request, but only on one condition. He said, 'I will stay here every day if you provide me with the charanamrit and mahaprasada.' Mother Yashoda, who would do anything to keep her son happy, agreed to Lord Shiva's condition, and since that day, Lord Shiva has resided in Nanda Bhavan in Nandgaon as Nandishvar Mahadeva

Chapter 18

Lord Shiva Gives the Best

A brahmana in Kashi Varanasi once prayed to Lord Shiva: 'I want to give my daughter in marriage, but I have no money. Please give me money.' Lord Shiva told him, 'Go to Vrindavana and meet with Srila Sanatana Gosvami, a great Vaishnava saint, who resides in Vrindavana near the old Sri Madana-Mohana temple. You can ask him to give you some wealth for your daughter's marriage.'

The brahmana went to Vrindavana on foot. Once there, he asked the local villagers for the whereabouts of a person named Sanatana Gosvami. As they all knew him, they pointed out his residence. Srila Sanatana Gosvami, wearing only a loincloth, used to go begging door-to-door for a small amount of prasada, and would take as his meal only one dry chapatti without salt. He would practise bhajans near the Yamuna River at Kaliya-Hrada, the former abode of the very poisonous snake Kaliya. Kaliya-Hrada was close to the Yamuna and therefore, its surrounding area was full of sand.

The brahmana arrived at Sanatana Gosvami's cottage and said, 'I went to Sankara Mahadeva, Lord Shiva, and he told me to meet you. He said you will give me some wealth for my daughter's marriage.' Sanatana Gosvami replied, 'I have no possessions. You can see that I have nothing but a loincloth.' Then he thought, 'Oh, Shiva cannot tell a lie. He is my friend.' Thinking of Lord Shiva and contemplating further, he remembered a wish-fulfilling jewel (touchstone) he had once disregarded and then forgotten. Then he told the brahmana, 'Go to the Yamuna and remove some of the sand, and there you will find a touchstone. It is somewhere in the sand, though I don't remember where.'

The brahmana found the jewel, touched it to iron, and the iron turned into gold. Ecstatic that Lord Siva had told him to come to Vrindavana, he thought with gratitude, 'My prayer has been answered by him.' On the way home, however, his greed for money increased and he began thinking, 'Why did Sanatana Gosvami keep the touchstone in the sand? It had no use there. He must have more valuable jewels.'

He thus returned, and Sanatana Gosvami asked him, 'Why have you come back?' He replied, 'I've come because I know that you have more valuable jewels than this.' Sanatana Gosvami then said, 'Go and throw the touchstone in the Yamuna.' The brahmana did so with all his power. Sanatana Gosvami told him to come closer and gave him the mantra, 'Hare Krishna Hare Krishna Krishna Krishna Hare Hare, Hare Rama Hare Rama Rama Rama Hare Hare'. He said, 'I do not have worldly jewels, but I have transcendental jewels. The jewel of Lord Krishna and Sri

Radha will come to you in a very short time. So remain here. Your daughter's marriage will take place automatically. Stay here and chant Hare Lord Krishna.' That brahmana followed his instruction and became an elevated saint.

Srila Sanatana Gosvami would go daily to see Sri Gopisvara Mahadeva at his temple. Once, in his older years, Sanatana Gosvami had a dream, wherein Gopisvara Mahadeva appeared and instructed him: 'Now that you are old, please do not go through so much trouble to see me.' Sanatana Gosvami replied, 'I will continue to come. I cannot change this habit.' Gopisvara Mahadeva said, 'Then I will come and stay near your residence, manifesting in Bankhandi.' The very next day, Sri Gopisvara Mahadeva appeared in Bankhandi, halfway between his original temple and Srila Sanatana Gosvami's residence. Seeing this, Sanatana Gosvami became overwhelmed with transcendental ecstasy, and from that day on, visited Bankhandi Mahadeva every day.

Wherever he was, Srila Sanatana Gosvami could not live without his beloved Lord Shiva—Gopisvara Mahadeva and Bankhandi Mahadeva in Vrindavana, Kamesvara Mahadeva in Kamyavana forest and Chakaleshvara Mahadeva in Govardhana.

Chapter 19

The Lover of Bhagavat

Shrimad Bhagavatam is the highest scripture that narrates the most auspicious and charming pastimes of the Supreme Lord Krishna and His various incarnations. These narrations are so fascinating that they attract even those personalities who are self-satisfied and detached from material affairs. Lord Shiva happens to be one such personality—he does not just relish hearing the pastimes of the Supreme Lord but also takes great pleasure in reciting them. The following episode of a great devotee's life proves this fact.

Once there lived an ardent devotee of Lord Krishna called Poonthaanam. He worshipped Lord Guruvayur, an ancient deity of Lord Krishna, also known as Guruvayoorappan, with all his heart and soul. People loved him for his beautiful Bhagavatam discourses.

There is a temple in North Kerala called Kottiyoor, the main deity in which is Lord Shiva. The temple was kept open only for a few days during the year and no human activities were permitted for the rest.

Once, Poonthaanam reached the Kottiyoor temple and had a bath in the holy river. He worshipped the compassionate Lord Shiva and stayed there for a few days.

Every day, he recited the Bhagavatam in front of the deity, and a large audience of several hundred people eagerly listened to his narration of the pastime found in the tenth canto's sixtieth chapter of Shrimad Bhagavatam, titled 'Lord Krishna Teases Queen Rukmini'. The gist of the pastime is as follows:

Lord Krishna decides to joke with His beloved wife, Queen Rukmini. He playfully asks her why she wanted to marry the Lord when She had better choices like King Sisupala, Salva, Jarasandha, etc.

Hearing this, just with the thought of not being with Lord Krishna, Queen Rukmini faints and the Lord consoles her.

When Poonthaanam finished reading this part of the chapter, he kept the bookmark at the end so that he could continue reciting from the next chapter the coming day.

The next day, to his surprise, he found the bookmark at the beginning of the same chapter.

So, Poonthaanam read the same part for the second time.

This was repeated for the rest of the days.

It was the last day to close the temple for the year.

Poonthanam finished the discourse and was returning from the temple with the other devotees. He had already walked some distance when he remembered that he had forgotten to bring the Bhagavatam with him and left it in the temple.

He hurried back, crossed the river and reached the entrance to the temple, which was closed. He found himself to be all alone.

But he could hear somebody reciting the same part of the chapter from the Bhagavatam inside the temple.

As he looked through the keyhole, he saw Lord Shiva himself reading from Poonthanam's Bhagavatam.

Mother Parvati and his other ganas (associates such as ghosts, hobgoblins etc) were listening with their eyes filled with tears of devotion.

Poonthaanam stood there motionless and heard the whole recitation.

In the end, Lord Shiva asked Mother Parvati, 'Did you like the Bhagavatam recitation?'

She replied, 'Yes, it was nice, but it was not as good as Poonthaanam's'.

Lord Shiva replied, 'Yes. That is true. I also like to hear Bhagavatam from Poonthaanam. That is why I placed the bookmark again and again at the beginning of the same topic every day.'

Hearing this, Poonthaanam felt so shaken up that he uttered the holy name of Lord Krishna loudly.

When he looked again, Lord Shiva and Mother Parvati had disappeared from his sight.

Chapter 20

Shivastak: A Beautiful Prayer
Composed by Lord Chaitanya

Lord Krishna, the supreme authority on all subjects and the source of all knowledge, appeared 500 years ago as Lord Chaitanya Mahaprabhu to teach the world the right way to perform devotional service and perfect our lives. While He visited various Lord Shiva temples during His tour of South India, through His conduct, He showed how Lord Shiva must be respected, worshipped or prayed to. Following is a beautiful prayer that He composed and gives a complete understanding of the real nature and position of Lord Shiva. We could recite it regularly and more so, on special days like Shivaratri or whenever we visit a Shiva temple.

(1)
namo namas te tri-dasheshvaraya
bhutadi-nathaya mrdaya nityam
ganga-tarangotthita-bala-chandra
chudaya gauri-nayanotsavaya

I perpetually offer obeisances unto you, the lord of the thirty primal devas, who is the original father of created beings, whose character is gracious, upon whose head, which is crested by the sickle moon, the Ganga springs and who are a festival for the eyes of Gauri, the fair goddess.

(2)
su-tapta-chamikara-chandra-nila padma-
pravalambuda-kanti-vastraih
sunritya-rangeshta-vara-pradaya
kaivalya-nathaya vrisha-dhvajaya

I offer my obeisances to you who resemble a moon of molten gold, who is dressed in garments coloured like a group of budding blue lotuses or lustrous rainclouds, who bestows the most desirable boon on your devotees by your delightful dancing, who offers shelter to those who seek to become one with the transcendental effulgence of Godhead and whose flag bears the image of the bull.

(3)
sudhamshu-suryagni-vilochanena
tamo-bhide te jagatah shivaya
sahasra-shubhramshu-sahasra-rashmi
sahasra-sanjittvara-tejase 'stu

I offer my obeisances to you who dispels darkness with your three eyes—the moon, the sun and fire—and thus cause auspiciousness for all the living entities of the

universe, and whose potency easily defeats thousands of
moons and suns.

(4)
nagesha-ratnojjvala-vigrahaya sharddula-
charmamshuka-divya-tejase
sahasra-patropari samsthitaya varangadamukta-
bhuja-dvayaya

I offer my obeisances to you, whose form is brilliantly
illuminated by the jewels of Anantadeva, the king
of snakes, who possesses divine potencies and is
clothed in a tiger skin, who stands in the midst of a
1000-petaled lotus and whose two arms are adorned by
lustrous bangles.

(5)
su-nupuraranjita-pada-padma ksharat-sudha-bhritya-
sukha-pradaya
vichitra-ratnaugha-vibhushitaya
premanam evadya harau vidhehi

I offer my obeisances to you who bestows happiness
on your servitors as you pour upon them the liquid
nectar flowing from your reddish lotus feet, upon which
charming ankle bells ring. Obeisances unto you who is
adorned by an abundance of gems. Please endow me
today with pure love for Shri Hari.

(6)

shri-rama govinda mukunda shaure
shri-krishna narayana vasudeva
ity adi-namamrita-pana-matta bhringadhipayakhila-
duhkha-hantre

O Sri Rama! O Govinda! O Mukunda! O Sauri! O Sri
Krsna! O Narayana! O Vasudeva! I offer my obeisances
unto you, Shri Shiva, who is the monarch ruling over all
the bee-like devotees who are mad to drink the nectar
of these and other innumerable names of Hari, and who
thus destroys all grief.

(7)

shri-naradadyaih satatam sugopya
jijnasitayashu vara-pradaya
tebhyo harer bhakti-sukha-pradaya
shivaya sarvva-gurave namah

I offer my respectful obeisances to you, Shri Shiva, who
is forever inquired of confidentially by Shri Narada
and other great sages, who very easily bestows boons
on them, who bestows the happiness of Hari-bhakti
on those who seek boons of you, who thereby creates
auspiciousness and is thus the guru of everyone.

(8)

shri-gauri-netrotsava-mangalaya
tat-prana-nathaya rasa-pradaya
sada samutkantha-govinda-lila
gana-pravinaya namo 'stu tubhyam

I offer my obeisances to you who is a festival of auspiciousness for the eyes of Gauri, who is the lord of her life-energy, who bestows rasa and is an expert in forever singing songs with an eagerness of the pastimes of Govinda.

|| The Result of Hearing this Prayer ||

etat shivasyashtakam adbhutam mahat
shrinvan hari-prema labheta shighram
jnana cha vijnanam apurvva-vaibhavam
yo bhava-purnah paramam samadaram

A person who lovingly hears with rapt attention this wonderful eightfold prayer to Shri Shiva can quickly gain a love for Lord Shri Hari, transcendental knowledge, the realization of that knowledge and unprecedented devotional potency.

Chapter 21

Rudra Gita

'A devotee who rises early in the morning and with folded hands chants these prayers sung by Lord Shiva, and gives facility to others to hear them, certainly becomes free from reactions to Karma.'

Shrimad Bhagavatam 4.24.78

Gita means the song and Rudra Gita means the song sung by Lord Shiva. Just like we have the Bhagavad Gita, the song sung by Lord Krishna, similarly, we have the Rudra Gita mentioned in the fourth canto, chapter 24 (text 33–79) of Shrimad Bhagavatam. It is considered extremely pious and auspicious to chant this special prayer and fulfil all desires. Even if we do not understand it fully, simply reciting this prayer will purify our hearts and bring us unlimited good fortune by removing all obstacles from our lives.

Even if we cannot recite the Sanskrit, we advise everyone to recite the translations of the verses as it is equally powerful. There is no difference. On someone's special day, we must do what makes them happy to get their favour. Since this prayer is most dear to Lord Shiva, if we recite it on Shivaratri, we shall get his special mercy.

Similar to the first chapter of the Bhagavad Gita, which gives the background to Lord Krishna's message that begins in the second chapter, it is important that we understand the background of the Rudra Gita too. So here it is.

The Background

Long ago, the ancient king Maharaj Barhishat, henceforward known as Prachinabarhi, ruled the world. He was ordered by Lord Brahma to marry the daughter of the ocean named Shatadruti. Shatadruti was incredibly beautiful and very young. When she was adorned with the proper garments and brought to the marriage arena, everyone was floored by her beauty.

The demons, the denizens of Gandharvaloka, the great sages, and the denizens of Siddhaloka, the earthly planets and Nagaloka, although highly exalted, were all captivated by the tinkling of her anklet's bells.

King Prachinabarhi had ten children through Shatadruti, all of whom were equally endowed with religiosity and became well-known as the Prachetas.

When the Prachetas were ordered by their father to marry and beget children, because of their pious and obedient nature, they accepted the words of their father with heart and soul. To practice austerities and penances for 10,000 years to become pure in order to carry out this sacred duty, they went towards the West. They wanted to worship Lord Vishnu and please Him to get His blessings.

While travelling, the Prachetas happened to see a great reservoir of water that seemed almost as big as the ocean. The water of this lake was so calm and quiet that it seemed like the mind of a great soul, and its inhabitants, the aquatics, appeared peaceful and happy.

In that great lake, there were different types of lotus. Some of them were bluish and some were red. Some of them grew at night, some in the day and some, like the indivara lotus flower, in the evening. Combined, the lotus flowers filled the lake so well that it appeared to be a great mine of such flowers. Consequently, on the shores, there were exotic birds like swans, cranes, chakravakas, karandavas and other beautiful water birds standing about.

There were various trees and creepers on all sides of the lake, with mad bumblebees humming all about them. The trees appeared to be filled with life due to the sweet humming of the bumblebees, and the saffron, which was contained in the lotus flowers, being thrown into the air. This created such an atmosphere that it appeared as though a festival were taking place.

As the Prachetas were admiring the beauty of the place, they suddenly heard vibrations from various drums and kettledrums along with other orderly musical sounds that were pleasing to the ear. In a few moments, they saw the most enchanting Lord Shiva, along with his associates, emerging from the lake.

The Prachetas felt fortunate to see Lord Shiva. His bodily lustre was just like molten gold, his throat was bluish and he had three eyes, which looked very mercifully upon his devotees. He was accompanied by many musicians, who were glorifying him. The Prachetas immediately offered their obeisances in great amazement and fell at the lotus feet of the lord.

Lord Shiva, being the protector of pious persons and persons of gentle behaviour, became very pleased with them. He thus began to speak as follows:

'You are all the sons of King Prachinabarhi and I wish all good fortune to you. I also know what you are going to do, and therefore, I am visible to you just to show my mercy upon you.'

He continued:

> *yah param ramhasah sakshat*
> *tri-gunaj java-samjnitat*
> *bhagavantam vasudevam*
> *prapannah sa priyo hi me*

(Shrimad Bhagavatam 4.24.28)

'Any person who has surrendered to the Supreme Lord, Krishna, the controller of everything— material nature as well as the living entity—is actually very dear to me.'

> *sva-dharma-nishthah shata-janmabhih puman*
> *virincatam eti tatah param hi mam*
> *avyakritam bhagavato 'tha vaishnavam*
> *padam yathaham vibudhah kalatyaye*

(Shrimad Bhagavatam 4.24.29)

'A person who executes his occupational duty
properly for 100 births becomes qualified to
occupy the post of Brahmā, and if he becomes
more qualified, he can approach Lord Shiva.
A person who has directly surrendered to Lord
Kṛiṣḥṇa, or Viṣḥṇu, in unalloyed devotional
service, is immediately promoted to the spiritual
planets. Lord Shiva and the other demigods
attain these planets after the destruction of this
material world.'

atha bhagavata yuyam
priyah stha bhagavan yatha
na mad bhagavatanam cha
preyan anyo 'sti karhichit

(Shrimad Bhagavatam 4.24.29)

'You are all devotees of the Lord, and as such
I appreciate that you are as respectable as the
Supreme Lord Himself. I know in this way that
the devotees also respect me and that I am dear
to them. Thus, no one can be as dear to the
devotees as I am.

Now I shall chant one mantra which is not only
transcendental, pure and auspicious, but it is the
best prayer for anyone who is aspiring to attain
the ultimate goal of life. When I chant this mantra,
please hear it carefully and attentively.'

'Rudra Gita'

The song sung by Lord Shiva

(1)
shri-rudra uvacha
jitam ta atma-vid-varya-
svastaye svastir astu me
bhavataradhasa raddham
sarvasma atmane namah

Lord Shiva addressed the Supreme Lord with the
following prayer: O Supreme Lord, all glories unto You.
You are the most exalted of all self-realized souls. Since
You are always auspicious for the self-realized, I wish
that You be auspicious for me. You are to be worshipped
by virtue of the all-perfect instructions You give. You
are the Supersoul; therefore, I offer my obeisances unto
You as the supreme living being.

(2)
namah pankaja-nabhaya
bhuta-sukshmendriyatmane
vasudevaya shantaya
kuta-sthaya sva-rochishe

My Lord, You are the origin of the creation by the lotus
flower which sprouts from Your navel. You are the
supreme controller of the senses and the sense objects
and You are also the all-pervading Vāsudeva. You are

most peaceful, and because of Your self-illuminated existence, You are not disturbed by the six kinds of transformations.

(3)
sankarshanaya sukshmaya
durantayantakaya cha
namo vishva-prabodhaya
pradyumnayantar-atmane

My dear Lord, You are the origin of the subtle material ingredients, the master of all integration as well as disintegration, the predominating deity named Sankarshana and the master of all intelligence, known as the predominating deity, Pradyumna. Therefore, I offer my respectful obeisances unto You.

(4)
namo namo 'niruddhaya
hsishkeshendriyatmane
namah paramahamsaya
purnaya nibhritatmane

My Lord, as the supreme directing deity known as Aniruddha, You are the master of the senses and the mind. I therefore offer my obeisances unto You again and again. You are known as Ananta as well as Sankarshana because of Your ability to destroy the whole creation by the blazing fire from Your mouth.

(5)
svargapavarga-dvaraya
nityam shuci-shade namah
namo hiranya-viryaya
chatur-hotraya tantave

My Lord, O Aniruddha, You are the authority by which
the doors of the higher planetary systems and liberation
are opened. You are always within the pure heart of the
living entity. Therefore, I offer my obeisances unto You.
You are the possessor of semen, which is like gold, and
thus, in the form of fire, You help the Vedic sacrifices,
beginning with *chaturhotra*.[70] Therefore I offer my
obeisances unto You.

(6)
nama urja ishe trayyah
pataye yajna-retase
tripti-daya ca jivanam
namah sarva-rasatmane

My Lord, You are the provider of the *pitṛlokas*[71] as well
as all the demigods. You are the predominating deity
of the moon and the master of all three Vedas. I offer
my respectful obeisances unto You because You are the
source of satisfaction for all living entities.

---

[70] Performed by four chief priests.

[71] The pitṛloka designates the celestial or nether world where the dead
forefathers (*pitṛs*) reside.

(7)
sarva-sattvatma-dehaya
visheshaya sthaviyase
namas trailokya-palaya
saha ojo-balaya ca

My dear Lord, You are the gigantic universal form that contains all the individual bodies of the living entities. You are the maintainer of the three worlds, and as such You maintain the mind, senses, body and air of life within them. I therefore offer my respectful obeisances unto You.

(8)
artha-lingaya nabhase
namo 'ntar-bahir-atmane
namah punyaya lokaya
amushmai bhuri-varchase

My dear Lord, by expanding Your transcendental vibrations, You reveal the actual meaning of everything. You are the all-pervading sky within and without, and You are the ultimate goal of pious activities executed both within this material world and beyond it. I therefore offer my respectful obeisances again and again unto You.

(9)
pravrittaya nivrittaya
pitri-devaya karmane

namo 'dharma-vipakaya
mrityave duhkha-daya cha

My dear Lord, You are the viewer of the results of pious
activities. You are inclination, disinclination and their
resultant activities. You are the cause of the miserable
conditions of life caused by irreligion, and therefore,
You are death. I offer You my respectful obeisances.

(10)
namas ta ashisham isha
manave karanatmane
namo dharmaya brihate
krishnayakuntha-medhase
purushaya puranaya
sankhya-yogeshvaraya cha

My dear Lord, You are the topmost of all bestowers of
all benediction, the oldest and supreme enjoyer amongst
all enjoyers. You are the master of all the worlds'
metaphysical philosophy, for You are the supreme
cause of all causes, Lord Kṛiṣhṇa. You are the greatest
of all religious principles, the supreme mind and You
have a brain which is never affected by any condition.
Therefore, I repeatedly offer my obeisances unto You.

(11)
shakti-traya-sametaya
midhushe 'hankritatmane
cheta-akuti-rupaya
namo vacho vibhutaye

My dear Lord, You are the supreme controller of the worker, sensory activities and results of sensory activities [karma]. Therefore, You are the controller of the body, mind and senses. You are also the supreme controller of egotism, known as Rudra. You are the source of knowledge and the activities of the Vedic injunctions.

(12)
darshanam no didrikshunsm
dehi bhagavatarchitam
rupam priyatamam svanam
sarvendriya-gunanjanam

My dear Lord, I wish to see You exactly in the form that Your very dear devotees worship. You have many other forms, but I wish to see Your form that is especially liked by the devotees. Please be merciful upon me and show me that form, for only that form worshipped by the devotees can perfectly satisfy all the demands of the senses.

(13–14)
snigdha-pravrid-ghana-shyamam
sarva-saundarya-sangraham
charv-ayata-hatur-bahu
sujata-ruchirananam
padma-kosha-palashaksham
sundara-bhru sunasikam
sudvijam sukapolasyaṁm
sama-karna-vibhushanam

The Lord's beauty resembles a dark cloud during the rainy season. As the rainfall glistens, His bodily features also glisten. Indeed, He is the sum total of all beauty. The Lord has four arms and an exquisitely beautiful face with eyes like lotus petals, a beautiful, highly-raised nose, a mind-attracting smile, a beautiful forehead and equally beautiful and fully decorated ears.

(15–16)
priti-prahasitapangam
alakai rupa-shobhitam
lasat-pankaja-kinjalka-
dukulam mrishta-kundalam
sphurat-kirita-valaya-
hara-nupura-mekhalam
shankha-chakra-gada-padma-
mala-many-uttamarddhimat

The Lord is very beautiful on account of His open and merciful smile and His sidelong glance upon His devotees. His black hair is curly, and His garments, waving in the wind, appear like flying saffron pollen from lotus flowers. His glittering earrings, shining helmet, bangles, garland, ankle bells, waist belt and various other bodily ornaments combine with conch shell, disc, club and lotus flower to increase the natural beauty of the Kaustubha pearl on His chest.

(17)
simha-skandha-tvisho bibhrat
saubhaga-griva-kaustubham

shriyanapayinya kshipta-
nikashashmorasollasat

The Lord has shoulders just like a lion's. Upon these
shoulders are garlands, necklaces and epaulettes, all of
which are always glittering. Besides these, there is the
beauty of the Kaustubhamaṇi pearl, and on the dark
chest of the Lord, there are streaks named Śrīvatsa,
which are signs of the goddess of fortune. The glittering
of these streaks excels the beauty of the golden streaks
on a gold-testing stone. Indeed, such beauty defeats a
gold-testing stone.

(18)
pura-rechaka-samvigna-
vali-valgu-dalodaram
pratisankramayad vishvam
nabhyavarta-gabhiraya

The Lord's abdomen is beautiful due to the three ripples
in the flesh. Being so round, His abdomen resembles
the leaf of a banyan tree, and when He exhales and
inhales, the movement of the ripples appears to be
incredibly beautiful. The coils within the navel of the
Lord are so deep that it appears that the entire universe
sprouted out of it and yet again wishes to go back.

(19)
hyama-shrony-adhi-rochishnu-
dukula-svarna-mekhalam

sama-charv-anghri-janghoru-
nimna-janu-sudarshanam

The lower part of the Lord's waist is dark and covered with yellow garments, and a belt bedecked with golden embroidery work. His symmetrical lotus feet, and the calves, thighs and joints of His legs are extraordinarily beautiful. Indeed, the Lord's entire body appears to be well built.

(20)
pada sharat-padma-palasha-rochisha
nakha-dyubhir no 'ntar-agham vidhunvata
pradarshaya sviyam apasta-sadhvasam
padam guro marga-gurus tamo-jusham

My dear Lord, Your two lotus feet are so beautiful that they appear like two blossoming petals of the lotus flower that grows during the autumn season. Indeed, the nails of Your lotus feet emanate such a great effulgence that they immediately dissipate all the darkness in the heart of a conditioned soul. My dear Lord, kindly show me that form of Yours which always dissipates all kinds of darkness in the heart of a devotee. My dear Lord, You are the supreme spiritual master of everyone; therefore, all conditioned souls covered with the darkness of ignorance can be enlightened by You as the spiritual master.

(21)
etad rupam anudhyeyam
atma-shuddhim abhipsatam

yad-bhakti-yogo 'bhayadah
sva-dharmam anutishthatam

My dear Lord, those who desire to purify their existence must always engage in meditation upon Your lotus feet, as described above. Those who are serious about executing their occupational duties and want freedom from fear must take to this process of bhakti-yoga.

(22)
bhavan bhaktimata labhyo
durlabhah sarva-dehinam
svarajyasyapy abhimata
ekantenatma-vid-gatih

My dear Lord, the king in charge of the heavenly kingdom is also desirous of obtaining the ultimate goal of life—devotional service. Similarly, You are the ultimate destination of those who identify themselves with You [aham brahmasmi]. However, it is very difficult for them to attain You, whereas a devotee can very easily attain Your Lordship.

(23)
tam duraradhyam aradhya
satam api durapaya
ekanta-bhaktya ko vanchet
pada-mulam vina bahih

My dear Lord, pure devotional service is even difficult for liberated persons to discharge, but devotional service alone can satisfy You. Who will take to other

processes of self-realization if he is serious about the
perfection of life?

(24)

yatra nirvishtam aranam
kritanto nabhimanyate
vishvam vidhvamsayan virya-
shaurya-visphurjita-bhruva

Simply by an expansion of His eyebrows, the invincible
time personified can immediately vanquish the entire
universe. However, the formidable time does not
approach the devotee who has taken complete shelter
at Your lotus feet.

(25)

kṣanardhenapi tulaye
na svargam napunar-bhavam
bhagavat-sangi-sangasya
martyanam kim utashishah

If one, by chance, associates with a devotee, even for a
fraction of a moment, he no longer is subject to attraction
by the results of karma or *jnana*. What interest then can
he have in the benedictions of the demigods, who are
subject to the laws of birth and death?

(26)

athanaghanghres tava kirti-tirthayor
antar-bahih-snana-vidhuta-papmanam

bhuteshv anukrosha-susattva-shilinam
syat sangamo 'nugraha esha nas tava

My dear Lord, Your lotus feet are the cause of all auspicious things and the destroyer of all the contamination of sin. I, therefore, beg Your Lordship to bless me with the association of Your devotees, who are completely purified by worshipping Your lotus feet and are merciful upon the conditioned souls. I think that Your real benediction will be to allow me to associate with such devotees.

(27)
na yasya chittam bahir-artha-vibhramam
tamo-guhayam ca vishuddham avishat
yad-bhakti-yoganugrhitam anjasa
munir vichashte nanu tatra te gatim

The devotee whose heart has been completely cleansed by the process of devotional service, and is favoured by Bhaktidevī, does not become bewildered by the external energy, which is just like a dark well. Being completely cleansed of all material contamination in this way, a devotee is able to understand very happily Your name, fame, form, activities, etc.

(28)
yatredam vyajyate vishvam
vishvasminn avabhati yat
tat tvam brahma param jyotir
akasham iva vistritam

My dear Lord, the impersonal Brahman spreads everywhere, like the sunshine or the sky. And that impersonal Brahman, which spreads throughout the universe and in which the entire universe is manifested, is You.

(29)
yo mayayedam puru-rupayasrijad
bibharti bhuyah kshapayaty avikriyah
yad-bheda-buddhih sad ivatma-duhsthaya
tvam atma-tantram bhagavan pratimahi

My dear Lord, You have manifold energies, and these energies are manifested in manifold forms. With such energies, You have also created this cosmic manifestation, and although You maintain it as if it were permanent, You ultimately annihilate it. Even though You are never disturbed by such changes and alterations, the living entities are disturbed by them, and therefore they find the cosmic manifestation to be different or separated from You. My Lord, You are always independent, and I can see this fact clearly.

(30)
kriya-kalapair idam eva yoginah
shraddhanvitah sadhu yajanti siddhaye
bhutendriyantah-karanopalakshitam
vede cha tantre cha ta eva kovidah

My dear Lord, Your universal form consists of all five elements—the senses, mind, intelligence, false ego

(which is material) and the Paramatma, Your partial
expansion, who is the director of everything. Yogis
other than the devotees—namely the karma-yogī and
jnana-yogi—worship You by their respective actions in
their respective positions. It is stated both in the Vedas
and in the *shastras* that are corollaries of the Vedas, and
indeed everywhere, that it is only You who are to be
worshipped. That is the expert version of all the Vedas.

(31)
tvam eka adyah purushah supta-shaktis
taya rajah-sattva-tamo vibhidyate
mahan aham kham marud agni-var-dharah
surarshayo bhuta-gana idam yatah

My dear Lord, You are the only Supreme Person, the
cause of all causes. Before the creation of this material
world, Your material energy remains in a dormant
condition. When Your material energy is agitated,
the three qualities—namely goodness, passion and
ignorance—act, and as a result the total material
energy—egotism, ether, air, fire, water, earth and all
the various demigods and saintly persons—becomes
manifest. Thus, the material world is created.

(32)
srishtam sva-shaktyedam anupravishtash
chatur-vidham puram atmamshakena
atho vidus tam purusham santam antar
bhunkte hrishikair madhu sara-gham yah

My dear Lord, after creating by Your own potencies, You enter within the creation in four kinds of forms. Being within the hearts of the living entities, You know them and know how they are enjoying their senses. The so-called happiness of this material creation is exactly like the bees' enjoyment of honey after it has been collected in the honeycomb.

(33)
sa esha lokan atichanda-vego
vikarshasi tvam khalu kala-yanah
bhutani bhutair anumeya-tattvo
ghanavalir vayur ivavishahyah

My dear Lord, Your absolute authority cannot be directly experienced, but one can guess by seeing the activities of the world, that everything is being destroyed in due course of time. The force of time is very strong, and everything is being destroyed by something else—just as one animal is being eaten by another animal. Time scatters everything, exactly as the wind scatters clouds in the sky.

(34)
pramattam ucchair iti kritya-chintaya
Pravriddha-lobham vishayeshu lalasam
tvam apramattah sahasabhipadyase
kshul-lelihano 'hir ivakhum antakah

My dear Lord, all living entities within this material world are mad after planning for things, and they are always busy with a desire to do this or that. This is due to uncontrollable greed. The greed for material enjoyment always exists in the living entity, but Your Lordship is always alert, and in due course of time, You strike him, just as a snake seizes a mouse and very easily swallows him.

(35)
kas tvat-padabjam vijahati pandito
yas te 'vamana-vyayamana-ketanah
vishankayasmad-gurur archati sma yad
vinopapattim manavash chaturdasha

My dear Lord, any learned person knows that unless he worships You, his entire life is spoiled. Knowing this, how could he give up worshipping Your lotus feet? Even our father and spiritual master, Lord Brahma, unhesitatingly worshipped You, and the fourteen Manus[72] followed in his footsteps.

(36)
atha tvam asi no brahman
paramatman vipashcitam
Vishvam rudra-bhaya-dhvastam
akutashcid-bhaya gatih

My dear Lord, all learned persons know You as the Supreme Brahman and the Supersoul. Although the entire universe is afraid of Lord Rudra, who ultimately

---

[72] The rulers of the universe.

annihilates everything, for the learned devotees, You are the fearless destination of all.

Concluding Instructions

(37)
idam japata bhadram vo
vishuddha nripa-nandanah
sva-dharmam anutisthanto
bhagavaty arpitashayah

My dear sons of the King, just execute your occupational duty as kings with a pure heart. Just chant this prayer fixing your mind on the lotus feet of the Lord. That will bring you all good fortune, for the Lord will be very pleased with you.

(38)
tam evatmanam atma-stham
sarva-bhuteshv avasthitam
pujayadhvam grinantash cha
dhyayantash chasakrid dharim

O sons of the King, the Supreme Lord, Hari, is situated in everyone's heart. He is also within your hearts. Therefore, chant the glories of the Lord and always meditate upon Him continuously.

(39)
yogadesham upasadya
dharayanto muni-vratah

samahita-dhiyah sarva
etad abhyasatadritah

My dear princes, in the form of a prayer I have delineated the yoga system of chanting the holy name. All of you should take this important *stotra* [prayer] within your minds and promise to keep it in order to become great sages. By acting silently like a great sage, giving your attention and reverence, you should practice this method.

(40)
idam aha purasmakam
bhagavan vishvaseik-patih
bhrigv-adinam atmajanam
sisṛkṣuḥ saṁsisṛkṣatām

This prayer was first spoken to us by Lord Brahma, the master of all creators. The creators, headed by Bhrigu, were instructed in these prayers because they wanted to create.

(41)
te vayam noditah sarve
praja-sarge prajeshvarah
anena dhvasta-tamasah
sisrikshmo vividhah prajah

When all the Prajapatis were ordered to create by Lord Brahma, we chanted these prayers in praise of the Supreme Lord and became completely free from all ignorance. Thus, we were able to create different types of living entities.

Benedictions

(42)
athedam nityada yukto
japann avahitah puman
achirach chreya apnoti
vasudeva-parayanah

A devotee of Lord Kṛiṣhṇa, whose mind is always absorbed in Him, who with great attention and reverence chants this stotra, will achieve the greatest perfection of life without delay.

(43)
shreyasam iha sarvesham
jnanam nihshreyasam param
sukham tarati dushparam
jnana-naur vyasanarnavam

In this material world, there are different types of achievement, but of all of them, the achievement of knowledge is considered to be the highest because one can cross the ocean of ignorance only on the boat of knowledge. Otherwise, the ocean is impassable.

(44)
ya imam shraddhaya yukto
mad-gitam bhagavat-stavam

adhiyano duraradhyam
harim aradhayaty asau

Although rendering devotional service to the Supreme
Lord and worshipping Him is very difficult, if one
vibrates or simply reads this Stotra composed and sung
by me, he will easily be able to invoke the mercy of the
Supreme Lord, Hari.

(45)
vindate purusho 'mushmad
yad yad icchaty asatvaram
mad-gita-gītāt supritach
chreyasam eka-vallabhat

The Supreme Lord is the most dear objective of all
auspicious benedictions. A human being who sings this
song sung by me can please the Supreme Lord. Such a
devotee, being fixed in the Lord's devotional service, can
acquire whatever he wants from the Supreme Lord.

(46)
idam yah kalya utthaya
pranjalih shraddhayanvitah
shrinuyach chravayen martyo
muchyate karma-bandhanaih

A devotee who rises early in the morning, and with
folded hands, chants these prayers sung by Lord Shiva,
and gives facility to others to hear them, certainly
becomes free from all bondage to fruitful activities.

(47)
gitam mayedam naradeva-nandanah
parasya pumsah paramatmanah stavam
japanta ekagra-dhiyas tapo mahat
charadhvam ante tata apsyathepsitam

My dear sons of the King, the prayers I have recited
to you are meant for pleasing the Supreme Lord, the
Supersoul. I advise you to recite these prayers, which
are as effective as great austerities. In this way, when
you are mature, your life will be successful, and you will
certainly achieve all your desired objectives without fail.

Chapter 22

Vaishnavas' Worship of Lord Shiva

Lord Krishna appeared 500 years ago in the holy land of Mayapur (about 130 km from Kolkata, West Bengal) as Lord Chaitanya. The specific purpose of this avatar was to show how to be a perfect devotee and an exemplary human being in general. He spent twenty-four out of forty-eight years of his life as a family man and twenty-four years as a *sannyasi*.[73] Out of these, he spent six years travelling throughout South India and spreading bhakti. He also showed, during these visits, how to honour Lord Shiva.

Chaitanya Charitamrita, the authorized biography on his life, describes how he visited innumerable temples of Lord Shiva during his travels in South India, and worshipped him with great devotion and love. On a mountain called Rishabh Hill, he even secretly met Lord Shiva and Parvati in the disguise of a brahman. They spent many days together discussing various topics. Goddess Parvati was cooking for Lord Chaitanya every day to His great satisfaction. Thus,

---

[73] A mendicant.

to worship Lord Shiva is an integral necessity in the lives of the great Vaishnavas. But their worship is for pure devotion whereas others worship Lord Shiva for material gain. Lord Shiva is the avatar of the Supreme Lord Himself and in his heart, has the highest level of pure devotion as a Vaishnava. But, practically 99 per cent of the society of India only understands Lord Shiva in his role as a demigod. What is the purpose of a demigod? To give material benedictions to those who are less intelligent and think that the goal of life is material prosperity. Lord Shiva is known as Ashutosh, which means that he is very easily pleased. As a demigod, as Ashutosh, he is obliged, if someone performs proper austerities, to give them whatever they want, irrespective of what the motive is.

It is said in the Shrimad Bhagavatam 12.13.16: 'Vaishnavanam yatha sambhuh': Lord Shiva is the best of all devotees or Vaishnavas. Therefore, all devotees of Lord Krishna are also devotees of Lord Shiva. In Vrindavana, there is a Lord Shiva temple called Gopishvara. While the gopis used to worship not only Lord Shiva but Katyayani or Durga as well, they aimed to attain the favour of Lord Krishna. A devotee of Lord Krishna does not disrespect Lord Shiva but worships Lord Shiva as the most exalted devotee of Lord Krishna. Consequently, whenever a devotee worships Lord Shiva, he does so to achieve the favour of Lord Krishna, and does not request material profit. In Bhagavad Gita (7.20), it is said that generally, people worship demigods for some material profit. Driven by material lust, they worship demigods, but a devotee never does so, for he is never driven by material lust. That is the difference between a devotee's respect for Lord Shiva and a demon's respect for him. The demon worships Lord Shiva, takes some benediction from him and misuses the benediction, only to be killed by the Supreme Lord later on.

The tenth canto of Shrimad Bhagavatam, chapter 88, describes the following pastime:

A demon named Vrikasur once met Sage Narada on the road. The wicked fellow asked him which of the three chief gods, Lord Brahma, Lord Shiva and Lord Vishnu could be pleased most quickly.

Narada told him, 'Worship Lord Shiva and you will soon achieve success. He quickly becomes pleased by seeing his worshipper's slightest good qualities—and quickly angered by seeing his slightest fault. He became pleased with ten-headed Ravana and Banasur when they each chanted his glories like bards in a royal court. Lord Shiva then bestowed unprecedented power upon each of them, but in both cases, he was consequently beset with difficulty as the demons caused great disturbance to the three worlds.'

Thus advised, the demon proceeded to worship Lord Shiva at Kedarnath by taking pieces of flesh from his own body and offering them as oblations into the sacred fire, which is Lord Shiva's mouth.

Vrikasur became frustrated after failing to obtain a vision of the lord. Finally, on the seventh day, after dipping his hair into the holy waters at Kedarnath and leaving it wet, he took up a hatchet and prepared to cut off his head. But at that very moment, the supremely merciful Lord Shiva rose out of the sacrificial fire, looking like the god of fire himself, and grabbed the demon's arms to stop him from killing himself, just as we would do. By Lord Shiva's touch, Vrikasur once again became whole.

Lord Shiva said to him, 'My friend, please stop, stop! Ask from me whatever you want, and I will bestow that boon upon you. Alas, you have subjected your body to great torment for no reason, since I am pleased with a simple offering of water from those who approach me for shelter.'

The benediction Vrikasur chose from the lord would terrify all living beings. Vrikasur said, 'May death come to whomever I touch upon the head with my hand.'

Upon hearing this, Lord Rudra seemed somewhat disturbed. Nonetheless, he vibrated 'om' to signify his assent, granting Vrikasur the benediction with an ironic smile, as if giving milk to a poisonous snake.

A problem manifested immediately, however. The demon had a crooked smile on his face and looked at Lord Shiva and announced his nefarious plan. He said, 'O Lord! Your wife is very beautiful and you don't appear to be a suitable match for her because of your shabby appearance. So I think she deserves a royal person like me. But as long as you are alive, I cannot have her. Thus, you must die. I will put my hand on your head and this way, kill you and also test the benediction you just gave me.'

The demon then tried to put his hand on the Lord's head. Lord Shiva was frightened because of what he had done. As the demon pursued him, Lord Shiva fled swiftly from his abode in the north, shaking with terror. He ran as far as the limits of the earth, the sky and the corners of the universe.

The great gods of the heavens could only remain silent, not knowing how to counteract the benediction. Then Lord Shiva reached the luminous realm of Vaikuntha, beyond all darkness, where the Supreme Lord Narayan is manifest. That realm is the destination of renunciants who have attained peace and given up all violence against other creatures. Going there, one never returns.

The Supreme Lord, who relieves His devotees' distress, had seen from afar that Lord Shiva was in danger. Thus, by His mystic yogamaya potency, He assumed the form of a brahmachari student, with the appropriate belt, deerskin, rod and prayer beads, and came before Vrikasur. The Lord's effulgence glowed brilliantly like fire. Holding kusha grass in His hand, He humbly greeted the demon.

The Supreme Lord sweetly said: 'My dear son of Shakuni, you appear tired. Why have you come such a great distance? Please rest for a minute. After all, it is one's body that fulfils all of one's desires. O mighty one, please tell us what you intend to do, if we are qualified to hear it. Usually one accomplishes his purposes by taking help from others.'

Thus questioned by the Lord in a language that poured down upon him like sweet nectar, Vrikasur felt relieved of his fatigue. He described to the Lord everything he had done.

The Supreme Lord said: 'If this is the case, We cannot believe what Lord Shiva says. Lord Shiva is the same lord of the *pretas*[74] whom Daksha cursed to become a carnivorous hobgoblin. Do you really think Lord Shiva's benedictions actually work? Ha-ha . . . they never work. I have seen it so many times.'

---

[74] Ghosts.

'What do you mean they never work?' the surprised demon asked.

The Lord replied, 'Yes. You will touch his head, nothing will happen, everyone will laugh at you, you will lose your reputation, you will be dishonoured and it will be worse than death. What will you do?'

'Now what should I do?' the demon enquired, panicking.

'Well, you should test to see if it works in a private place before you make a big embarrassment of yourself,' the bewitching Lord cleverly suggested. 'O best of the demons, if you still have any faith in him because he is the spiritual master of the universe, then without delay put your hand on your head and see what happens. If the words of Lord Shambhu prove untrue in any way, O best of the demons, then kill the liar so he may never lie again.'

Bewildered by the Lord's enchanting, artful words, foolish Vrikasur, without realizing what he was doing, placed his hand on his head.

Instantly, his head shattered as if struck by a lightning bolt, and the demon fell dead. From the sky were heard cries of 'Victory!' 'Obeisances!' and 'Well done!'

The celestial sages and other higher beings from the heavens rained down flowers to celebrate the killing of Vrikasur. Lord Shiva was thus out of danger.

The Supreme Lord then addressed Lord Shiva: 'Just see, O Mahadeva, My lord, how this wicked man has been killed by his sinful reactions. Indeed, what living being can hope for good fortune if he offends exalted saints? What to speak of offending the lord and spiritual master of the universe?'

Lord Shiva is duty-bound to give material benedictions, whether it's good for you or not if you approach him in his role as a demigod or devata. But people are not very inclined to worship Lord Hari. Why? Because Lord Krishna does not give you what you want, He gives you what you need. 'Hari' means the one who steals. If it is good for us to have lots of money and great mystic powers, Lord Hari will give us mystic powers and great wealth, as he did for King Yudhishtir, King Ambarish, King Priyavrat and so many other great personalities. But if it is not good for us, we can worship Him for money and we may end up with nothing.

Lord Krishna says in the Shrimad Bhagavatam (10.88.8):

shri-bhagavan uvacha
yasyaham anugrihnami
harishye tad-dhanam shanaih
tato 'dhanam tyajanty asya
svajana duhkha-duhkhitam

'Lord Krishna said that if I especially favour someone, I gradually deprive him of his wealth. Then the relatives and friends of such a poverty-stricken man abandon him. In this way, he suffers one distress after another.'

Lord Krishna says, 'My supreme compassion upon My devotee is sometimes that I take everything away so that the devotee has no pride left. He just cries out for Me helplessly. Hey Krishna! Hey Govinda! Then at that time, he is ready to receive my divine love, pure bhakti.'

This is why we find many people approach the demigod aspect of Lord Shiva as he easily gives material benedictions. But if we approach his aspect of the great Vaishnav, he will give us the greatest benediction of bhakti. Therefore, we find in the Srimad Bhagavatam that Lord Shiva gives those who are materialistically inclined whatever benedictions they want. But we find that Lord Shiva is always directing those who are sincere in understanding the absolute truth and their path of liberation to the worship of Lord Narayana, as in the case of the Prachetas, the sons of King Prachinabarhi. The fifth canto of the Bhagavatam describes that they approached Lord Shiva, who taught them beautiful songs that praised Lord Narayana when he saw that they cared for nothing of this world. They truly wanted the highest benediction. If they asked for mysticism, he would have given them great powers of control. They asked for the highest goal of life and the highest liberated state. Lord Shiva taught them beautiful personal prayers in the glorification of Lord Hari. Thus, he acted as spiritual master by giving them the highest boon—what was closest to his heart— bringing them to the devotional service of Lord Krishna. This is why we find so many devotees of Lord Krishna, who were earlier devotees of Lord Shiva.

Conclusion

To consider Lord Shiva or Lord Brahma on the same level as Lord Vishnu is an offence. At the same time, to consider Lord Shiva as different or independent from Lord Vishnu is also an offence. Therefore, Vaishnavas offer Lord Shiva all due respect as the topmost devotee of Lord Vishnu. On the holy occasion of Mahashivaratri, devotees may pray to Lord Shiva to help them progress on the path of Lord

Krishna bhakti swiftly. This is the greatest benediction that Lord Shiva is very keen to offer to all living entities. After all, it was Lord Shiva who guided the great saint Tulsidas to write Ramayana (Ramcharitmanas). It was he who inspired the great Vallabhacharya (founder of Pushti Marg) and Narsingh Mehta (the most famous bhakti saint from Gujarat) towards Lord Krishna bhakti, and it was he who helped the Prachetas attain the favour of Lord Vishnu. He has done it in the past and continues to guide sincere practitioners even today with the exhibition of his supreme mercy.

Chapter 23

The Secret Shiva

Few and fortunate know that Lord Shiva secretly appeared in this world around 538 years ago. Not in the sense that he was hiding somewhere from the eyes of the world, but that he hid his real identity from the rest of the world to assist the Supreme Lord in His mission of teaching bhakti through His example as a devotee.

Whenever the Supreme Lord Shri Krishna or any of His incarnations appear to re-establish dharma in this world, many of His associates also appear to assist Him. Thus, Lord Shiva also must appear in some capacity.

When the Lord appeared as Lord Ram, Lord Shiva appeared as Hanuman and served him dutifully. Whenever we remember Ramayana, Hanuman's pastimes of service to the Lord seem to supersede that of the Lord Himself.

In 1486, when Lord Krishna appeared as Lord Chaitanya in the holy land of Mayapaur (West Bengal), Lord Sadashiv from the spiritual realm incarnated as the great Advaita Acharya. In fact, it was only upon his call of love out of compassion for all in this world that Lord Krishna made His descent.

We have previously discussed how Lord Sankarshana (the expansion of Lord Krishna) gives rise to two personalities, Lord Maha-Vishnu and Lord Sadashiva. Advaita Acharya was the combined incarnation of both.

Some associates of the Lord appeared before Him to set the stage for His advent and Advaita Acharya was one of them. Many associates appeared around the Lord's appearance and many have kept appearing even after He returned to His supreme abode.

To discuss the entire life of Shri Advaita Acharya would be beyond the scope of this book and make it voluminous, but here I make a humble attempt to present his life in brief. For more details, I would request you to read the famous Chaitanya Bhagavat and Chaitanya Charitamirta, the authorized biographies of Lord Chaitanya.

Advaita Acharya appeared fifty to sixty years before Lord Chaitanya's advent. He was born in 1434 in Nabagram, Bengal, to Shri Kubera Pandit and Shrimati Nabha Devi, both of whom were committed to the devotional service of the Lord, on the seventh day of the waxing moon in the month of Magh. His parents were originally inhabitants of Nabagram village near Shri Hatta, but later moved to Shantipur near Nabadwip-Mayapur, the future birthplace of the Lord Chaitanya, on the banks of the holy Ganga.

According to Gaura-Gannodesh Dipika, a scripture that reveals the original identities of those who appeared in Lord Chaitanya's pastimes, Advaita Acharya's father Kuber was none other than the incarnation of the famous

Kuber, the treasurer of the heavenly gods and an associate of Lord Shiva.

When Kubera Pandit and Nabha Devi disappeared, Advaita went to Gaya on the pretext of performing the appropriate rituals of mourning, and thence continued on a pilgrimage tour of all of India's holy places. When he came to Vrindavan, he became absorbed in the worship of Lord Krishna. It was here that he discovered the deity of Shri Madan Mohan or Madan Gopal. He later entrusted this deity to the care of a Choube brahman[75] in Mathura before continuing his pilgrimage tour. It was this very same deity that was later served by Srila Sanatan Goswami and named Madan Mohan. The first ever temple built in Vrindavan about 500 years ago was the beautiful Madan Mohan temple right on the banks of Yamuna. After some time, through his meditation, Advaita Acharya was able to understand that Lord Krishna was about to appear in Nabadwip. So he returned to Nabadwip.

Advaita Acharya had two wives—one was named Sri, the other Sita. He had six sons, one of whom, Achyutananda, is described in the Gaura-Ganoddesha-Dipika (87–8) as the incarnation of Kartikeya, the son of Lord Shiva.

Advaita Acharya also had two residences—one in Shantipur and the other in Mayapur, not far from what was to be the home of Lord Chaitanya. He accepted the great Shri Madhavendra Puri as his spiritual master (Guru).

Being the incarnation of the most compassionate Lord Shiva, his heart was greatly pained at seeing that the people of the world were devoid of any devotion to Lord

---

[75] A particular caste of brahmanas.

Vishnu and were, as a consequence, greatly suffering the pains of material life. Overwhelmed with compassion, he began to teach the Bhagavad Gita and Bhagavat, explaining that the goal of life was to engage in devotional service to Lord Krishna.

In the fifteenth century, the land of Nabadwip was the high seat of learning. Students from all over the world would travel there to study under the best. There were scholars everywhere in the area, who were found teaching, debating, carrying books and busy learning various subjects. Unfortunately, due to the influence of this age of Kali, Navadwip was filled with materialism. People were so happy and content living in their great riches with their big, big degrees of learning that they became intoxicated with false pride, prestige, facilities and sensory gratification.

Nobody was interested in giving up the material life and taking shelter in the Supreme Lord. The whole town was filled with people performing rituals for various demigods, making offerings simply for their own material sense gratification. There were big elaborate pujas to Goddess Durga for material life while others were worshipping Manasa Devi, the goddess of serpents. People would spend lavish sums of money for entertainment and the weddings of their children. They would sometimes offer animals and blood to the various devas. And although Chakravartis, Misras, Bhattacharyas and other high categories of learned scholars existed, and recitations of Bhagvatams, Upanishads and scriptures happened everywhere, not even one mention of the word bhakti could be found. The kirtan of the holy name of Lord Krishna could be heard nowhere.

Hare Krishna, Hare Krishna, Krishna Krishna
Hare Hare, Hare Rama,
Hare Rama, Rama Rama Hare Hare.

No one had any interest in the Hari Katha—the beautiful narrations of the pastimes of the Supreme Lord. People were so infatuated and intoxicated by material existence that it broke the hearts of the devotees.

Materialistic people find it appealing when they see other people enjoying themselves, but when a devotee of the Lord, who is actually situated in the highest truths, sees someone just wallowing in opulence, wealth, high learning and big families, he simply weeps, pitying that person for his condemned condition and forgetting his eternal treasure of love for Lord Krishna.

The leader of all devotees of the time was Sri Advaita Acharya. His heart was burning to see the condition of the people of this world in Kaliyuga.

Every day, all the devotees would assemble at Advaita Acharya's house. Wherever they looked, they only saw materialism and ignorance and saw no devotion to God. So, when they took shelter in his house, they exclusively performed three activities. They worshipped Lord Krishna, they talked about Him and loudly chanted His holy names.

Hare Krishna, Hare Krishna, Krishna Krishna Hare Hare, Hare Rama, Hare Rama, Rama Rama Hare Hare.

The four brothers Shrivasa Pandita (the incarnation of Narada Muni), Shri Rama, Shrinidhi, and Shripati, were constantly having kirtan and discussions on Lord Krishna's pastimes, which the people of Navadwip found to be a disturbance and hated. They would complain,

They're keeping us up all night with this loud chanting. We need good sleep. Why? So we have full energy to make money and enjoy more and more. And this Shrivasa and his brothers, they have become so mad. They're chanting so loudly. Why don't they chant silently? Chanting loudly, they will wake Mahavishnu, who is in his yoga sleep, and He will become so angry that He will destroy the universe. And what about the king of the Muslims? When he hears that Hindus are chanting the names of God loudly, he will come with his soldiers, arrest us all, plunder us and kill us! So before this happens, we should kick this Shrivasa and his family out of Nabdwipa. We should break his house into pieces and throw those pieces in the Ganga. We cannot tolerate this!

The devotees were very unhappy hearing insults and blasphemies constantly.

Shri Advaita Acharya, with his heart melting in compassion, made a vow. He resolved that through his prayers, he would bring the Supreme Lord Krishna down to this earth and deliver everyone by spreading the Sankirtan movement—the devotional singing of Lord Krishna's holy names and the recommended spiritual practice for this yuga. He began to fast. Throughout the day in Navadwip Dham on the banks of the Ganga and sometimes in Shantipur, he would worship the Supreme Lord with the holy water of the Ganga and tulsi leaves. He shed tears of love for God and of compassion for all souls profusely. With his limbs trembling, he would call out for the Lord to appear in this world and give his mercy freely to everyone. He cried out for Lord Krishna with such devotion that his voice penetrated all the layers of material existence, all the way to the spiritual world, where it reached the heart of Lord Krishna Himself. Thus, by the power of the love and compassion of Shri Advaita Acharya, the Supreme Lord made his descent on to this world on a full moon day in 1486, the month of Phalguna in the holy land of Mayapur. And while it is only because of Lord Chaitanya's supreme mercy that the bhakti movement is spreading across the world through His teachings and associates, it would not have been possible without the efforts of Shri Advaita Acharya, the merciful Sadashiva.

Advaita Acharya lived for 125 years and passed away in 1559. The place on the banks of the Ganga where Shri Advaita Acharya worshipped the Shalagram Shila (a form of Lord Vishnu) and called out to the Lord to descend to the world, is known today as Babla. A temple has been built in memory of Advaita Acharya's pastimes there.

In deep gratitude, we bow down to Shri Advaita Acharya, Lord Sadashiv, for bringing the Lord into this world, who blessed us with the all-glorious, all-auspicious path of bhakti—devotional service to the Supreme Lord Krishna—thus helping us realize the goal of life, leading to our good fortune. Had it not been for him, we would probably not even be reading this book. The events that occurred 600 years ago are the ultimate cause of the manifestation of this book. I hope it has served its purpose by bringing everyone close to the real purpose of life, which is the realization of God, Lord Krishna.

Acknowledgements

I humbly bow down and express my immense gratitude to the divine Sage Vyasa, who painstakingly and carefully compiled all the Vedic scriptures that are this book's main source of content.

My most humble obeisances and thanks to my *param*[1] guru His Divine Grace A.C. Bhaktivedanta Swami Srila Prabhupada (founder Acharya of ISKCON) and my guru His Holiness Radhanath Swami for making the teachings of Vyasadev so accessible and understandable, thus giving me an opportunity to come up with the idea to write this book.

I am forever grateful to the editorial team at Penguin—Gurveen, Anushree and Aparna—for their hard work and patience through the entire process of publication. They were extremely kind and encouraging towards all my efforts.

Credit is also due to our dear devotees Sonal Anand, Harneet, Jharna and Sneha for fine-tuning the content at the final stages, thus taking a lot of burden (of love) off my head.

May Krishna and Lord Shiva bless all these sincere souls with the best that They have to offer.

---

[1] Supreme.

Scan QR code to access the
Penguin Random House India website